American Dreams, Global Visions

Dialogic Teacher Research
With Refugee and Immigrant Families

Sociocultural, Political, and Historical Studies in Education
Joel Spring, Editor

American Dreams, Global Visions

Dialogic Teacher Research
With Refugee and Immigrant Families

Edited by

Donald F. Hones
University of Wisconsin–Oshkosh

Routledge
Taylor & Francis Group
New York   London

Maps included in this book were drawn by
Idus Ebeigbe and reprinted with permission.

First published by Lawrence Erlbaum Associates, Inc., Publishers
10 Industrial Avenue
Mahwah, New Jersey 07430

Transferred to digital printing 2010 by Routledge

Routledge

270 Madison Avenue
New York, NY 10016

2 Park Square, Milton Park
Abingdon, Oxon OX14 4RN, UK

Cover design by Kathryn Houghtaling Lacey

Library of Congress Cataloging-in-Publication Data

American dreams, global visions : dialogic teacher research with
    refugee and immigrant families / edited by Donald F. Hones.
        p. cm.
    Includes bibliographical references and index.
ISBN 0-8058-3707-8 (cloth : alk. paper)
ISBN 0-8058-3708-6 (pbk. : alk. paper)
1. Immigrants—Wisconsin—Oshkosh—Case studies. 2. Refugees
    —Wisconsin—Oshkosh—Case studies. 3. Action research in
    education—Wisconsin—Oshkosh—Case studies.   I. Hones,
    Donald F.
JV7123.O74 A44   2002
305.9'0691'0977564—dc21   2002019890
                                                    CIP

10   9   8   7   6   5   4   3   2   1

In memory of my father,
Donald F. Hones, Sr.,
who dreamed of a world without borders

Contents

Tables and Maps

Preface

Marcel Donovan dropped into this world of probes, bright lights, and injections on a Friday afternoon in February. The bravery of his mother, the aerobics instructor—like the sunny disposition of the midwife and the gently reassuring nature of the attending nurse—could not dispel the gnawing feeling inside me that something was wrong, and not with the baby: As I observed the nurses pinch and poke him, watched them take his footprints twice (too soon to start a file with the FBI), listened to the intermittent, high-pitched beeps coming from the "baby warmer" machine, and watched Marcel struggle and fight back like a born rebel, I began to understand that we have much to learn about welcoming newcomers to our world.

Oshkosh, Wisconsin, the setting for these postnatal experiments, is named for a Winnebago chieftain noteworthy for being alive when Europeans took control of his tribe's ancestral lands. Two statues of Chief Oshkosh can be found in Menominee Park. He stands, cast in bronze, in the middle of a picnic ground—young, strong, and good-looking, staring out with dark eyes toward Lake Winnebago. Nearby, in another representation, he slouches at the entrance to the popular "Little Oshkosh" playground, a stereotypical wooden Indian, broken, old, and ridiculous in a stovepipe hat and frock coat. He looks sad as the children rush past, and I want to speak to him, to hear his story, to ask him why:

> Oshkosh,
> Why?
> Why did you choose the White Man's Road?
> Why did you compromise?
> Was it to save your people?
> For disease and despair claimed many

The good German farmers took what was left of the land
and
in gratitude
they named a beer after you.

Life in Oshkosh would not always be a picnic for the immigrants, either. Protesting the unfair labor practices of lumber barons, German and Southern European workers were instrumental in waging a bitter strike in 1898, a strike that still divides this largely working class town. The struggle of working families remains close to the surface here, as corporate flight has cost the area many of its better paid factory jobs. When they learn I am living here, friends and acquaintances often exclaim, "Oshkosh b'gosh!" Yes, the company is still here, but all those cute little clothes are made somewhere down in Mexico now where workers can be paid a lot less, thus insuring higher corporate profits.

The local loss of jobs, though evidently part of a corporate master plan, left many working-people casting about for someone to blame. In the 1970s, refugees from Laos began to resettle in Oshkosh, bringing with them a Hmong culture, language, and kinship patterns that were rarely understood or approved of by the now entrenched European-Americans. Few knew why they were here, or the part they played in support of the United States during the Vietnam War. Many would have denied them welfare benefits given to refugees, or begrudged them any language services for their children in schools. Even today, when a full implementation of welfare-to-work policies cause many Hmong parents to work two jobs to support their families, the stereotype of their being "welfare cheats" who "drive around in fancy cars" remains.

As successive groups of immigrants, including Kurds, Bosnians, Kosovars, and Mexicans, have made Oshkosh and surrounding communities their home, intolerance and racism have grown apace; sometimes it as overt as a swastika on a family's door, but more often it is casual, perhaps unconscious, such as an insistence on not allowing refugees and immigrants to speak their native languages with friends at school. Few third- or fourth-generation Americans understand our nation's integral part in effecting the political and economic contexts that have brought these newcomers to this land: our support of Saddam Hussein during his war with Iran and his gassing of Kurdish villages; our reluctance to get involved as the catastrophe of ethnic cleansing in the Balkans intensified in the early 1990s; our long history of political and economic conflict, subjugation, and intolerance toward the Mexican people. Refugees and immigrants carry with them intimate knowledge of these cross-national contexts and the effects on their lives, and could teach us much. However, we must take the time to listen, and give them the opportunity to speak.

In effect, Oshkosh is a typical American city, filled with hardworking, somewhat conservative inhabitants who are reluctant to change their ways or openly embrace newcomers. They want their children to grow up with a certain set of values, and are suspicious of multiculturalism creeping into the curriculum. There are good people here, people who will lend a neighbor a hand, people who will work together to build a playground for kids. I believe there are people here who are ready for the challenge of opening their minds, and their ears, and their hearts, to the lives of their distant cousins in the human family. What they need are teachers who can help initiate a dialogue between the various elements of our increasingly diverse community.

THE CHALLENGE

This book is about *dialogic teacher research* with immigrant and refugee families. What is dialogic teacher research? It encompasses methods that are at once ethnographic, participatory, and narrative; it seeks to engage researchers and participants in dialogues that shed light on economic, political, social, and cultural relationships, and seeks to represent these dialogues in texts; it seeks to extend these dialogues to promote broader understanding and social justice in schools and communities (Freire, 1970; Giroux, 1997; Hones & Cha, 1999; Moll & Greenberg, 1990; G. Spindler & L. Spindler, 1994). Since the spring of 1998, my students at the University of Wisconsin–Oshkosh have conducted dialogic teacher research with families as part of their course work. Several positive outcomes have accompanied this research: Our preservice and current teachers have enriched their understanding of immigrant languages and cultures. Members of the families have benefited from the knowledge of the schools, English lessons, and other study support offered by preservice teachers. Friendships have formed that have lasted far beyond the 14 weeks of our course together. The teachers have also developed ethnographic portraits of families, and they have tried to present these portraits in a variety of forms. In this book, there are sections of dialogue between teachers and family members; at other times, poetry is used to present the words of participants and writers; and the stories told by families have been prepared as picture books for use in school classrooms.

This book is about dialogue between immigrants, refugees, and teachers. It is about American dreams of those who have lived here for a few generations and those who have just arrived. It is about the global visions shared when American teachers learn from the worldly experiences and perspectives of those who have struggled to survive wars, famines, natural disasters, and global economics. Many of the economic and political conflicts that bring immigrants and refugees to the United States have their roots in our nation's own policies: Hmong refugees, who make up the largest single newcomer group in northeastern Wisconsin, are in the United States as a direct result of their support for a covert U.S. war inside Laos during the Vietnam era. Similarly, refugees from Kurdistan were supporters of U.S. military involvement against Iraq. In both cases, when U.S. forces pulled out, their Hmong and Kurdish allies had to leave as well, or face imprisonment and death. Mexican immigrants, on the other hand, arrive without official refugee status, and yet their economic livelihood in their homeland has been compromised by their country's involvement in the North Atlantic Free Trade Agreement (NAFTA). Kosovar refugees, victims of ethnic cleansing policies, have had the opportunity to return home, in part because of U.S. support for international pressure on Serbia in recent years. Teachers need to become familiar with the political, economic, and sociocultural contexts of these immigrant and refugee lives, and the role of the United States in influencing these contexts in positive and negative ways.

OVERVIEW

Part I of this book, "Dialogic Teacher Research," provides the foundation for the immigrant and refugee narratives to follow. Chapter 1, "Dialogues of Cultural and Educational Change," suggests a way to bring together narrative, cultural, and critical dialogues about education at the beginning of the 21st century. Accompanying these three dialogues are three multifaceted cultural roles for teachers: cultural storytellers, cultural healers, and cultural workers. Chapter 2, "Dialogic Teacher Research With Family Narratives," describes the context in which this book took form, as part of a class project in our university Teachers of English to Speakers of Other Languages (TESOL) program. Students were engaged in dialogic teacher research with refugee and immigrant families, and the challenges, findings, and benefits of this research are highlighted.

Part II of this book provides ethnographic portraits of four immigrant families. Each chapter begins with a country and cultural group profile, and ends with suggestions for further reading and relevant Web sites. Chapter 3, "A Hmong Family," describes the life of Chan Lor and his family, refugees from Laos, as shared in interviews with Faye Van Damme, a preschool English as a second language (ESL) teacher. Chapter 4, "A Mexican Family," describes the life and experiences of Angela Gonzales and her family, recent immigrants from Mexico, as shared with Judy Mehn, a graduate student, and Maya Song-Goede, an ESL teacher at the school Ms. Gonzales' son attends. Chapter 5, "An Assyrian Family," describes the experiences of six siblings in the Dawood family, orphaned refugees from Iraqi Kurdistan, who shared their story with Katie Hinz, an undergraduate student. Chapter 6, "A

Kosovar Family," describes the experiences of the Sutaj family of refugees from Kosovo, as shared with Jessica Wade-Martinez, an undergraduate student and co-worker at their relative's restaurant.

Part III, "Extending the Dialogue," provides a synthesis of major themes in the preceding chapters and suggests implications for educators and policymakers. Chapter 7, "Extending the Dialogue: Pathways for Change," provides examples of how dialogic teacher research with immigrant families can inspire changes in teaching, curriculum, and school–community relations.

As a teacher educator at the dawn of a new century, I feel that forging a stronger connection between teachers, newcomers, and their families is one of the greatest challenges facing schools in the United States. As Giroux (1997) suggested, this is often a challenge of *remembrance*: For teachers to remember their own ethnic and linguistic past, and their own family's passage to a new world; for children, the first generation growing up in America, to gain the self-esteem that comes when they value the remembrances of their elders; for all of us in this nation, and in our world community, to learn from the experiences of refugees and immigrants, living proof of the drastic political and economic changes going on around our globe.

In the aftermath of the terrorist attack of September 11, 2001, the United States has engaged in military strikes against Afghanistan, one of the world's poorest countries. Hundreds of thousands of refugees are once again on the move, seeking food, shelter, and peace. Meanwhile, within the United States, civil liberties are being curtailed in the name of a "war on terrorism." Many who oppose wars of vengeance, global exploitation of people, and environmental degradation have felt compelled to keep silent during these troubling times. Yet now, more than ever, we are challenged to find ways to engage in dialogue about our lives together, about our common relationship with the earth and all who live on it.

The alternative is to acquiesce to a world where lives are divided, degraded, and discarded in the pursuit of profit.

ACKNOWLEDGMENTS

This book was the product of many hands. Katie Hinz, Judy Mehn, Maya Song-Goede, Faye Van Damme, and Jessica Wade-Martinez deserve special thanks for their time, energy, and ideas in writing their excellent stories, as well as reviewing the book as a whole. I would like to thank Idus Ebeigbe for the maps in this volume. Gratitude is due to those who shared their lives with us—the Lors, Gonzales, Dawood, and Sutaj families. Their voices, openness, and insight make this book possible. I had the pleasure of working once again with Naomi Silverman of Lawrence Erlbaum Associates and

Joel Spring of New School University, who were supportive of this work from the outset. Naomi offered many valuable suggestions on an early draft that helped provide focus for the volume. Lori Hawver, Stacey Mulligan, and Barbara Wieghaus helped guide this book through the final editing process. Thanks also to Lois Spitzer, University of Nebraska–Lincoln, for reviewing the manuscript. Finally, I thank Kathleen, Orion, Ariana, and Marcel, for their patience and understanding when I was off somewhere, writing.

—Donald F. Hones

I

Dialogic Teacher Research

1

Dialogues of Cultural and Educational Change

To exist, humanly, is to name *the world, to change it.*

—Freire (1970, p. 76)

The new millennium finds Americans experiencing rapid cultural change. Hundreds of thousands of workers have been displaced by downsizing and corporate flight as companies seek more profits in the capitalist global economy. Omnipresent advertising in the mass media has prepared people from an early age to consume, place high value on material things, and buy on credit. Those Americans who find their earnings won't support a lifestyle they aspire to, and facing children who seem to have lost, somehow, traditional values, have become worried and frustrated with the apparently drastic cultural changes altering the land of their birth. Some, encouraged by politicians, talk show hosts, and other leaders of public opinion, have blamed their economic and social problems on an increasingly visible, vocal, and politically active non-White population.

Along with established African-American, Mexican-American, Asian-American, and Native-American communities, recent immigration has contributed to the growth of the non-White population of the United States. Approximately 10% of all Americans today were born outside the United States (U.S. Census Bureau, 2000). These newcomers, many of whom are refugees from wars, revolutions, and drastic economic change, differ from previous generations of immigrants in that most come from Latin America and Asia, and relatively few from Europe.

By 1976, there were more than twice as many immigrant nationalities represented in the United States than there had been in 1920 (Fuchs,

3

1990). By 2010 people, who trace their origins to Africa, Asia, and Latin America will be in the majority, and their children have already transformed the demographics of American schools (Giroux, 1997; see also Table 1.1, this chap.). Working with this culturally and linguistically diverse student population is a teaching force that remains predominantly European-American and middle class (Cochran-Smith, 1995; Delpit, 1987).

Those who have sought to address the cultural transformation of American schools through multicultural and bilingual education have been criticized by conservative scholars, who blame cultural pluralists for the "disuniting of America," and have called for a renewed focus on "American" cultural literacy and "traditional American values" (Hirsch, 1988; Schlesinger, 1991). Okihiro (1994) summarized this conservative critique as follows:

> In its stress on racial, gender, class and sexual inequality, in its insistence on identity and self-definition, the *margin* has led the nation astray, far from the original formulations that made the Republic great, has created instead balkanized enclaves—ghettos—and even worse, has stirred up social conflict and "culture wars." Without a center, things have fallen apart. (pp. 149–150)

TABLE 1.1

Immigrant and Refugee Americans: Regions of Origin and Size of Foreign-Born Population (U.S. Bureau of the Census, 2000)

Region	Population (Estimate)	Percentage of Total
Asia	8,397,093	28%
Latin America[a]	15,501,472	51%
Europe	4,768,602	15%
Other[b]	1,854,186	6%
Total	30,520,323	100.00

- 13,339,456, or 43%, of the foreign-born population has entered the United States since 1990.

- By region, the foreign-born population is concentrated in with West (40%) and South (27%), with smaller populations in the Northeast (22%) and Midwest (11%).

- 17% of the foreign-born population lives below the poverty level; 22% of those born in Latin America live below the poverty level.

[a]The majority of those from Latin America are from Mexico.
[b]Other includes those from Africa, Canada, and Bermuda.

Things have fallen apart before, and rapid cultural change is not a stranger to this hemisphere: Several hundred years of European colonization of the Americas, with the consequent genocidal wars, destruction of religions, elimination of languages and ways of life, and enslavement of indigenous and African others, provides a particularly drastic example of such cultural change. Yet, American society is clearly in the process of another great transformation, and it is apparent to many that we are becoming a "hybrid" or "mestizo" culture. Carlson (1996) wrote that such a transformation requires us to move beyond the colonial legacy of education in the modern era, which divided the world into the civilized and the savages. Postcolonial education involves

... a shift away from seeing racial or cultural identities as separate and distinct categories of difference and toward seeing them as interrelated and informed by one another. The postmodern, postcolonial subject is a hybrid subject, constructed as one culture rubs up against another and produces something new and emergent. (p. 135)

Historically, teachers and schools have been positioned to first address societal change resulting from the influx of new cultural groups with differing beliefs and values from those of the dominant culture. Just as newcomers to America have to make adjustments and learn to get along in a new environment, so must teachers and schools. How are teachers' concepts of culture challenged and transformed by their work in multicultural settings?

A growing body of scholarly literature suggests that this transformation occurs through a dialogical process (Bakhtin, 1981; Freire, 1970; McLaren, 2000; Moraes, 1996; Shor, 1992; Wink, 2000). According to Sarris (1993), it is through dialogue that we come to understand persons of other cultures as well as ourselves:

In understanding another person and culture you must simultaneously understand yourself. The process is ongoing, an endeavor aimed not at a final and transparent understanding of the Other or of the self, but at continued communication, at an ever-widening understanding of both. (p. 6)

Three ongoing scholarly dialogues address the lives and cultural work of teachers. The first part of this essay explores the *narrative dialogue*, the use of narrative research as a mode of inquiry which allows teachers' lives and voices to enter research texts and public forums on education. The second part of this essay examines the *cultural dialogue*, the conceptions of culture that influence the work of teachers, students, families, and communities in the educational process. The third part of this essay presents the *critical dialogue,* which challenges the power relationships within society that influence and are influenced by schooling. Finally, these narrative, cultural and critical dialogues suggest possible cultural roles for teachers in their work at the critical juncture of family, school, and society.

THE NARRATIVE DIALOGUE

There is an increasing use of narrative inquiry within the broader field of educational research. Phillips (1994) traced the history of educational inquiry from naturalistic social science to hermeneutics to narratives, a history marked by "the gradual erosion of the positivist model of man ... and the struggle to replace it with a model that more adequately reflects what we humans take to be the nature of ourselves as thinking, feeling, and sometimes rational creatures" (p. 14). Much importance in qualitative research today is placed on meaning-making and folk psychology (Bruner, 1990). Bellah, Madsen, Sullivan, Swidler, and Tipton (1985) suggested that social science, when utilizing interpretive methods, can become "a form of self-understanding or self-interpretation" as it "seeks to relate the stories scholars tell to the stories current in the society at large" (p. 301). The integration of historical, sociological, psychological, and cultural perspectives to describe the lives of others allows for what Rabinow and Sullivan (1987) called the return to the *hermeneutical circle,* or "circle of meaning" that is a goal of interpretive social science.

Narrative research takes hermeneutics one step further by arguing that people understand their lives and explain their lives through stories, and these stories feature plots, characters, times, and places. Polkinghorne (1995) argued that the narrative is "the linguistic form uniquely suited for displaying human existence as situated action" (p. 5). Clandinin and Connelly (1994) suggested that the reconstructed stories of people's lives are a fundamental educational tool: "People live stories, and in the telling of them reaffirm them, modify them, and create new ones ... Stories ... educate the self and others, including the young and those, such as researchers, who are new to their communities" (p. 415).

Moreover, noted scholars in many fields have suggested that the study of individual lives over time is indispensable for social inquiry (see, e.g., Clausen, 1993; Cremin, 1988). In anthropology, Rabinow (1977) and Crapanzano (1980) explored the difficulties and possibilities of combining life histories with cultural analysis; in psychology, life history has often been part of the study of personality development over time (Erikson, 1950; White, 1952); and in sociology, individual life histories have been woven into community mosaics (Becker, 1970; Terkel, 1972). Such biographical work encompasses Mills's (1959) contention that "Man is a social and an historical actor who must be understood, if at all, in close and intricate interplay with social and historical structures" (p. 158).

In an extensive survey of narrative research in the field of education, Casey (1995) suggested several reasons why this mode of interpretive inquiry has wide appeal among educational researchers at the end of the 20th century: Narrative research reverses "the academic trend toward deterministic economic analysis and reproductive cultural studies of schooling" (p. 214) by focusing on human agency and the ability of individuals to creatively construct their lives within social and historical contexts. In a study of the lives of six preschool teachers, Ayers (1989) highlighted the meaningfulness of autobiographies that intersect with the multiple biographies of students and others:

> Autobiography then is an act of self-penetration and self-understanding. We recognize the presentness of the autobiographer, the way in which memories and recollections must have meaning for now, and how that meaning can help shape intentionality and wide-awakedness for the future. And ... autobiography can be particularly salient for teachers who exist not only in the matrix of self and world but also at the crossroads of so many other biographies. (p. 19)

In discussing literacy lives of students and teachers, Meyer (1996) reminded readers that "our initial frame of any story is our own story. And our own story is dependent on our relationship with those around us" (p. 121; see also Bateson, 1990). Such a relationship is built on the trust that comes through the sharing of stories (Barone, 1995) and on the creation of collaborative, respectful research relationships (Schulz, 1997). McBeth and Horne (1996) presented an example of such a collaborative research relationship by composing a dialogue of their life history work together.

Much narrative research focuses on the lives of ordinary people, individuals whose lives are in part defined by racial, class and gender boundaries constructed by the dominant culture. Casey (1995) suggested that by "celebrating" the lives of diverse individuals and diverse histories, such narratives offer an alternative to a traditional canon shaped by a history of "great White men" (p. 215). In a similar vein, Goodson (1992) argued that the study of teachers' lives offers a way to contest the concept of power and knowledge as held and produced by those in positions of political, social, and economic power:

> Studying teachers' lives should represent an attempt to generate a counter-culture which will resist the tendency to return teachers to the shadows; a counterculture based upon a research mode that above all takes teachers seriously and seeks to listen to the teacher's voice. (p. 10)

Butt, Raymond, McCue, and Yamagishi (1992) suggested that, through collaborative autobiographical studies, teachers and educational researchers can contribute to ongoing dialogues about scholarly inquiry, professional knowledge, and reform. They present the case studies of two Canadian teachers who constructed personal/professional autobiographies as tools of reflection on their life, their work, and their vision of the future. The authors argue that the legitimation of teacher knowledge and the fostering of collaborative relationships between teachers and researchers are fundamentally issues of power, and that "moving from existing alienating practices to teacher- and school-based approaches must be regarded as an issue of teacher empowerment and emancipation" (pp. 56–57).

Moreover, narratives offer contrasting ways in which to address the social and psychological disruptions that characterize our times. At the level of the TV talk show, wrote Casey (1995), "telling one's story becomes exhibitionism, and listening to another's becomes voyeurism." However, narrative also offers a "way to put shards of experience together, to (re)construct identity, community, and tradition, if only temporarily" (p. 216). Paley's (1995, 1977) autobiographical accounts of life as a "White teacher" in multicultural settings presents one such effort to reconstruct a sense of community among diverse teacher and student identities. Wasley (1994) presented five stories of teachers struggling to understand their changing identities as they change classroom practice. *Naming Silenced Lives*, edited by McLaughlin and Tierney (1993), presented several ways in which narratives can highlight the search for identity and a public voice of teachers, community members, and others. Gitlin and Meyers (1993) argued that "while teachers have stories to tell about educational policy and practice, these stories are rarely given a forum in the public domain" (p. 51). Gitlin and Meyers (1993) presented the story of Beth, a teacher who is able to write about and reexamine her own life as a teacher. By telling her story, Beth is able to critically examine her own role in the classroom, as well as to begin to question and "protest what is narrow and constraining about schooling" (p. 68). In a narrative study of seven teachers in Canada, Goodson and Cole (1993) broadened the definition of professional knowledge to include knowledge of the micropolitical and contextual realities of the school as a workplace. McLaughlin (1993) developed a course involving multicultural education, critical theory, and Navajo-English language curriculum development to the Navajo and White staff at an elementary school on the Navajo reservation. Participants developed autobiographical narratives that they analyzed through the lenses of cultural conflict, choice, self-identity, self-esteem, and voice. Through their examination of personal narratives, participants began to ask important questions about the cultural context of their work:

Are my assumptions about teaching, learning, and curriculum contributing to the domination and subordination of the students and their local communities? Even against my best intentions, am I replicating the impositions of ... dorm aides, teachers, foster parents, or the simple misunderstandings and injustices of the Anglo trader? (McLaughlin, 1993, p. 114)

Foster (1993) presented the lives of several African-American teachers and their efforts to "socialize Black children toward a 'double consciousness' by cultivating in them the individual resolution, mettle, moral strength, and clarity of purpose while simultaneously developing strong racial consciousness and pride" (p. 171).

As can be seen by the aforementioned examples, the narrative dialogue, focusing as it does on lives in context, is inextricably bound up with culture. Culture influences the lives of teachers, students, and others, and an understanding of the ongoing American cultural dialogue is needed to make sense of those lives.

THE CULTURAL DIALOGUE

One's culture plays an enormous role in shaping one's sense of identity. Geertz (1987) defined the culture of a people as "an ensemble of texts, themselves ensembles, that the anthropologist strains to read over the shoulders of those to whom they properly belong" (p. 239). Rabinow and Sullivan (1987) suggested a dialogical approach to understanding culture: "Culture—the shared meanings, practices, and symbols that constitute the human world—does not present itself neutrally or with one voice. It is always multivocal and overdetermined, and both the observer and the observed are always enmeshed in it" (p. 7).

G. Spindler and L. Spindler (1990) examined the American cultural dialogue and its transmission, suggesting that Americans must move beyond individualism and the identification of an enemy to greater sense of community responsibility; that the real enemy to the American cultural dialogue is inequity, fostered by "individualistic, self-oriented success, the successful drive for wealth by individuals uncommitted to the public good" (p. 165). G. Spindler and L. Spindler (1990) argued that at the center of the American cultural dialogue are mainstream values such as individualism, personal achievement, and a belief in progress, yet "various forms of biculturalism ... may constitute viable adaptations to the need to 'get along' in America at the same time that ethnic pride dictates a retention of self-orientation within one's own culture of origin" (p. 37). G. Spindler and L. Spindler (1994) offered *cultural therapy* as an answer for educators who would address the multiple conflicts that divide individuals, families, and ethnic and socioeconomic groups in society. Cultural therapy is a process of healing that involves several steps. First, participants (teachers, students, families, and others) must acknowledge that cultural conflicts exist and make the nature of such conflict explicit. Next, participants must address how this conflict involves their *enduring* and *situated* selves. The enduring self is a sense of continuity with one's past and social identity, whereas the situated self is pragmatic, contextualized, and adaptable to changing conditions of everyday life. The enduring self can become endangered when it is "violated too often or too strongly by the requirements of the situated self ... [This] certainly occurs as children and youth of diverse cultural origins confront school cultures that are antagonistic to the premises and behavioral patterns of their own culture" (p. 14). Finally, cultural therapy addresses the requirements for *instrumental competence* in schools, which includes academic skills as well as the social skills suitable for participation in the larger society. For example, teachers would be encouraged to prepare members of minority cultures for the requirements of test taking, while acknowledging that test taking is predicated on the ritualized norms of Anglo-oriented schools.

Ogbu (1982, 1991) proposed that some cultural minorities may have an easier time adapting to the dominant culture in school than others. Ogbu distinguishes between "voluntary" minorities, such as immigrants who chose to come to the United States and tend to place more value on and trust in schooling, as a way to make it in the new country; and "involuntary" minorities, such as African Americans, many Mexican Americans, and Native Americans, who were forced into the U.S. social system by means of slavery, war, and conquest. Involuntary minorities tend to view their options as already limited by society, and schooling as a waste of time; in effect, they often adopt a "resistance" stance toward school (see also Anyon, 1995; Entwistle, 1977). For such involuntary minorities, occasional educational "success" for a few individuals often leads to alienation from both their own cultural group and the dominant culture, relegating them to the no-man's land of Rodriguez's (1982) "scholarship boy" (see also Phelan & Davidson, 1993).

The quandary teachers who work with nondominant groups face, according to Gee (1990), is how to recognize and honor the "discourse communities" of students while at the same time giving them the tools to operate in the dominant discourse community, what Delpit (1987) refers to as "the rules of power." Gee (1990) advocated that teachers teach students to "make do" in the dominant discourse, learning the literacy tools that will allow them to participate effectively in the larger society without requiring them to "reject" their own community (see also Heath, 1983). Sleeter and Grant (1991) suggested the need for teachers to map the cultural terrains of power in the classroom, whereas Trueba and Delgado-Gaitan (1988) and Pai (1990) sought to uncover the cultural content and processes of schools.

These educational researchers are, according to Gibson (1988), suggesting that immigrants can adapt to the dominant culture without being forced to assimilate; that they need not be forced into dichotomies such as Rodriguez's (1982) public and private identities, with their first language and culture relegated to the home.

Important research on the relationship between schools and minority language communities draws on Vygotsky's (1978) cognitive theories, which suggest that the young learn about the world through interaction with more knowledgeable members of the community and culture, and that meaning is socially constructed and mediated through language. Moll and Greenberg (1990) extended Vygotskian theory to argue that *funds of knowledge*—valuable resources for everyday living—are exchanged among the immigrant home and community, and that these "funds" are indispensable resources for schools. Moreover, Moll and Greenberg (1990) argued that connecting schools with the homes of minority language students will give students and teachers new learning opportunities:

> We are convinced that teachers can establish, in systematic ways, the necessary social relations outside classrooms that will change and improve what occurs within the classroom walls. These social connections help teachers and students to develop their awareness of how they can use the everyday to understand classroom content and use classroom activities to understand social reality. (pp. 345–346)

Despite this evidence that diverse communities can contribute to the educational process, Diaz Soto (1997) chronicled how an active, educationally supportive Puerto Rican community found that their voices went unheard as the schools dismantled a bilingual education program. Their bilingual children, according to Diaz Soto (1997), were denied educational, civil, and human rights:

> Legal mandates in our nation may not be sufficient to protect children's educational civil rights, nor as in this case, the political will and voices of bilingual families. Coercive forces of power continued to exacerbate xenophobic perspectives that have effectively foreclosed the Latino/a children's opportunity to participate in a bilingual program. (p. 91)

Like Diaz Soto (1997), Moll and Greenberg (1990), Montero-Sieburth and Gray (1992) recognized the value of collaborative inquiry in multicultural school settings between university researchers and school teachers:

> Diversity is not based on the numbers of students or teachers who represent different ethnic groups in urban schools, but rather lies in the kinds of social relationships and interactions that occur. Teachers need to celebrate their own diversity before they can celebrate that of their students. (p. 134)

Recognizing the diversity within the teaching force itself provides an inclusive starting point for dialogues about culture in research projects in schools. Hauser (1994), for example, focused on the cultural consciousness-raising aspects of G. Spindler and L. Spindlers' (1990, 1994) work, yet rejects the term *therapy* because Hauser feels it implies that "people are not able to solve their own problems and that someone else has to get inside their head to help" (p. 171). Rather, she proposes a process of *reflective cultural analysis* as a group instructional technique. Hauser undertook a staff development project among majority Euro-American teachers working at a school in California where close to half the students came from homes where various immigrant cultures were practiced and where English was not the first language. Through seven sessions with school staff, Hauser attempted, with limited success, to engage teachers in reflective analysis of cultural differences, relate their personal educational histories to concepts of culture, consider personal episodes of cross-cultural contact and conflict within the school, and explore avenues for achieving more cultural congruence.

Dialogue about culture and cultural change, is by its nature *critical dialogue*. If the cultural dialogue is to include Americans in all their diversity, all must be allowed to speak and to be heard. Freire (1970) wrote:

> Dialogue cannot occur between those who want to name the world and those who do not wish this naming—between those who deny other[s] the right to speak their word and those whose right to speak has been denied them ... [Humans] are not built in silence, but in word, in work, in action-reflection. (p. 76)

The critical dialogue describes the work of educators who wish to encourage students, teachers and others, especially those who have been marginalized because of their race, class, or gender, to critically examine their lives in the contexts of cultural change and conflict, social and economic power, and democratic pluralism.

THE CRITICAL DIALOGUE

The critical dialogue brings together issues of voice and diversity raised in the narrative and cultural dialogues, adding to them the issue of power. Peters and Lankshear (1996) suggested several reasons why cultural difference and cultural conflict have surfaced as issues in school and society:

> Western culture is seen to have undergone a process of accelerated cultural differentiation, especially since the Second World War. The liberal myth of a common culture, or form of life, which functioned to assimilate difference

and otherness has split into a seemingly endless proliferation of subcultures and groups. The revitalization of indigenous cultures is seen as an important part of this differentiation process. With a new respect for the integrity of traditional cultures—a respect given only grudgingly under the increasing weight of a moral force deriving historically from philosophies of decolonization—Western liberal states have begun processes of redressing past grievances and of recognizing languages, epistomologies, aesthetics, and ethics different from "their own." (p. 3)

The dominant metanarratives of the past are questioned and replaced by counternarratives of resistance (Giroux, Lankshear, McLaren, & Peters, 1996). Cultural studies, according to Giroux (1996), challenged the notion that teachers are mere transmitters of culture; rather, they must "be educated to be cultural producers, to treat culture as an activity, unfinished and incomplete" (p. 104).

Levinson and Holland (1996) wrote that there are many ways in which "the notion of an 'educated' person is culturally constructed within, outside, and against dominant, elite- and state-sponsored institutions" (p. 23). Levinson, Foley, and Holland (1996) drew on the work of Bourdieu (1977), yet they move beyond his rather narrow concentration on "high" culture to look at ways in which "educated persons" are culturally produced through the interaction of minority and dominant cultures. They offer a series of case studies, which examine schools as sites for negotiated cultural production among Mesquaki youth in White schools (Foley, 1996), Chicano educators in south Texas (Trujillo, 1996), Aymara student teachers in Bolivia (Luykx, 1996), and elsewhere. These case studies suggest that "school knowledge can be empowering for subordinate groups as long as it respects, and even draws upon, the cultural resources of those groups" (Levinson & Holland, p. 24).

Covello and Horton were educators who prepared immigrants, workers, civil rights activists, and others to challenge the dominant constructions of culture and power. In their lives and work they embodied a concern for social justice, democracy and making peace between the school, the home, and society. As a principal in East Harlem in the first half of this century, Covello (1958) encouraged the use of bilingual teachers who could speak the languages of diverse children and parents, opened the school to community groups, and organized across ethnic groups on common issues of socioeconomic justice. Tyack and Hansot (1982) wrote that Covello "believed that the school itself should mobilize neighborhood people to bring about social justice" (p. 210). Horton (1990) founded Highlander School, which has been a center for labor, civil rights, and community education since the 1930s. Horton (1990) argued that part of the educational work of schools and teachers is to help channel decision-making powers and responsibilities to members of the community:

If we are to have a democratic society, people must find or invent new channels through which decisions can be made. Given genuine decision-making
powers, people not only learn rapidly to make socially useful decisions, but
they will also assume responsibilities for carrying out decisions based on
their collective judgment ... to convince people who have been ignored or
excluded in the past that their involvement will have meaning and that their
ideas will be respected. (p. 134)

Diaz Soto (1997) suggested the serious contemporary need for such
channels for democratic decision making on educational matters in minority language communities. Analyzing the connection between knowledge, power, and identity in English as a second language (ESL)
classrooms, Cummins (1994) wrote that "subordinated group students
are disabled educationally and rendered 'voiceless' or silenced in very
much the same way that their communities have been disempowered
(often for centuries) through their interactions with societal institutions,"
and that students will succeed to the extent that patterns of interaction in
school "actively challenge societal power relations" (p. 46).

Teachers, according to Kincheloe (1993), must be aware of the ways in
which "socioeconomic and ideological forces construct consciousness
while at the same time observing how individual children, real-life students, respond to this construction" (p. 215). Ladson-Billings (1995) argued for a culturally relevant pedagogy that moves beyond a focus on
student achievement to help students "accept and affirm their cultural
identity while developing critical perspectives that challenge inequities
that schools (and other institutions) perpetuate" (p. 469).

CULTURAL ROLES OF TEACHERS

The preceding narrative, cultural, and critical dialogues about education con-
tain within them several assertions about teachers' cultural roles. The narrative dialogue asserts that the teacher is a *storyteller*, a collector of stories, and
an interpreter; the cultural dialogue asserts that the teacher must be a *healer*,
who can prepare students for life in the dominant culture without stripping
away their own cultural understandings; the critical dialogue builds on the
previous two dialogues, adding that the teacher, as *cultural worker*, must address issues of power in the classroom and in society. These three possible
roles, and their variations, are now discussed in more detail.

The Cultural Storyteller

Teachers as *biographers* develop and value their own cultural autobiography as a reflective tool and a source of professional knowledge (Ayers,

1989; Goodson, 1992). Moreover, they can encourage the telling and sharing of diverse student autobiographies as part of their practice and curriculum (Barone, 1995; Paley, 1995). This may help teachers to better understand the "circles of meanings" (Rabinow & Sullivan, 1987) reflected in the lives of students and communities. The study of life stories provides a format for improving teacher–student relationships through awareness of cultural difference, an important component in cultural therapy as practiced by G. Spindler and L. Spindler (1990, 1994) or in "family-based multicultural education" as recommended by Walker-Moffat (1995).

The teacher is a *ethnographer* or *interpreter* when seeking to understand the lives of students and their families and to interpret these lives to the dominant culture (Delgado-Gaitan & Trueba, 1991). Teachers address their own sense of cultural identity as well as participate in direct intercultural experiences in the wider community (Zeichner, 1993). The use of ethnographic techniques such as participant observation and field notes can help teachers document these experiences for later reflection with colleagues (Moll, 1992). They also provide a basis for teachers to interpret the dominant culture to all students, and especially those who come to school with different cultural understandings. Finally, the work of interpretation provides an ongoing format for the continual personal and professional growth of teachers who might otherwise be mired in curricula that is not of their own creation and removed from the life experiences of their students.

The Cultural Healer

The teacher as cultural *therapist* seeks first to come to an understanding of her own sense of culture as manifested in her lived experiences, and then to understand the cultural understandings of students (G. Spindler & L. Spindler, 1994). This is therapy, then, for both teachers, students and society. In his foreword to *Pathways to Cultural Awareness* (1994), Trueba wrote:

Could anyone really question the universal need for healing? The daily stories about hatred, cruelty, war, and conflict dividing nations, regions, states, cities, and neighborhoods reveal clearly the open wounds and hurts of many. We all carry profound emotional injuries that affect another deeper sense of self and the ability to recognize who we are individually and collectively. (p. viii)

The teacher as therapist can help students to manage the stress involved in multiple cultural conflicts between home, school, peer groups, and society (Phelan & Davidson, 1994).

Beyond the need for healing, the teacher as *power linguist* recognizes the importance of minority students to maintain ties to their cultural and linguistic communities while learning the tools necessary to participate in the dominant discourse (Delpit, 1987; Gee, 1990; Gibson, 1988).

The Cultural Worker

When teachers see their role as defenders of an established "American" culture against perceived threats posed by minority cultural understandings, they may take on the role of the meta-story teller or *border guard* (e.g., Bloom, 1987; Hirsch, 1988; Schlesinger, 1992). Other public figures (e.g., talk show hosts, politicians, movie producers) can be border guards in the negative sense, in that their interpretations and representations of the world can negatively affect the way that cultural groups interact.

According to Giroux (1997), when teachers challenge the metanarratives by encouraging the development of student counternarratives, they take on the role of *border crossers*. Giroux describes the work of border pedagogy:

> ... to engage the multiple references that constitute different cultural codes, experiences, and languages ... not only to read these codes critically but also to learn the limits of such codes, including the ones they use to construct their own narratives and histories ... [to] engage knowledge as a border crosser, as a person moving in and out of borders constructed around coordinates of difference and power. (p. 147)

The difference between the work of the border guard and the border crosser can be seen in the former's unreflective acceptance to the prescribed authority of custom and the latter's struggle for remembrance: Giroux (1997) wrote: "Remembrance is directed more toward specificity and struggle, it resurrects the legacies of actions and happenings, it points to the multitude of voices that constitute the struggle over history and power" (p. 154).

Here, then, in the role of the border crosser, the three dialogues come together: The border crosser commits him or herself to remembering and to helping students to remember their own histories of struggle; values diverse cultural and linguistic understandings of the world; and prepares students with the critical tools to address the unequal distribution of power in society.

SUMMARY

The United States has far to go in achieving a society where all people are treated with dignity and respect regardless of their color, gender or socioeconomic background. Nevertheless, Greene (1996) suggested that, through dialogue and a "passion for pluralism," (p. 167) our nation can become more of a home and less of a battleground:

> Many of us ... for all the tensions and disagreements around us, would reaffirm the value of principles like justice and equality and freedom and commitment to human rights, since without these we cannot even argue for the decency of welcoming. Only if more and more persons incarnate such principles, choosing to live by them and engage in dialogue in accord with them, are we likely to bring about a democratic pluralism and not fly apart in violence and disorder. (p. 167)

The narrative, cultural, and critical perspectives on education reviewed in this chapter suggest that the cultural work of teachers can be central to achieving a societal dialogue about who we would like to be as Americans. As cultural storytellers for our society, teachers can use the study of their own lives to help them better understand the lives of students, and, by facilitating the telling of student lives, help us to better understand who we are as a people. Strategically placed between the home, the school, and society, teachers have sometimes exacerbated cultural conflicts in students' lives, yet they are also in a position to do the work of cultural healing that is necessary in our often wounded society. Finally, as cultural workers, as producers of culture, teachers can encourage students to create, and to critically address unequal power constructions in their lives.

2

Dialogic Teacher Research With Family Narratives

Through the hotel window, the hubbub of Manhattan filters in with the late afternoon sun. In the hazy half light, the features of Chan Lor, a Hmong refugee from Laos, are revealed. He is sitting in a stiff chair near the front of a small conference room, next to his wife, Khou, and Faye Van Damme, a preschool teacher. Like the slow, whispering voice of fire, his words flow, gaining strength and surpassing the haunting sounds of the *qeng*, which emanate from a tape player in the back of the room. He becomes silent, and Faye Van Damme, teacher and researcher of family lives, begins to weave her own story in with a translation of the events reported by Chan, focusing on an eventful day in their respective lives: January 15, 1983. On that day, Faye celebrated her 17th birthday in Wisconsin, while a world away, Chan attempted the dangerous crossing of the Mekhong River:

> There is much laughter and frivolity as friends and family enter the balloon- and streamer-filled house. Games are played, gifts are opened, and cake is eaten, all in the name of fun.
> There is no laughter, only seriousness and dead quiet. It is a 15-mile walk to the shores of safety. It is unknown who is going to die. Many lose their feet from walking on land mines. Shirttails are held, boats are loaded, and strangers are trusted, all in the name of freedom. (Van Damme, p. 39, this volume)

Faye Van Damme, Chan and Khou Lor are first-time visitors to New York, newcomers and new voices in the world of academic conferences. They bring with them a story of many border crossings, a story that is a weaving of two lives, a story about bridging the gap between schools and the homes of bilingual students and families.

For the past 3 years, students in our Teachers of English to Speakers of Other Languages (TESOL) program have carried out dialogic teacher research projects carried out with immigrant and refugee families. The objectives of this project were to improve the understanding of pre- and in-service teachers of the lives of immigrant families, and to facilitate a dialogue between the home and the school. *Dialogic teacher research* encompasses methods that are at once ethnographic, participatory, and narrative; it seeks to engage researchers and participants in dialogues that shed light on economic, political, social, and cultural relationships, and to represent these dialogues in texts; it seeks to extend these dialogues to promote broader understanding and social justice in schools and communities (Freire, 1970; Giroux, 1997; Hones & Cha, 1999; Moll & Greenberg, 1990; G. Spindler & L. Spindler, 1994). At the heart of dialogic teacher research are the *cultural roles of teachers*, the theoretical framework discussed in chapter 1 which guided the development of this project: Teachers have the potential to be cultural storytellers, cultural healers, and cultural workers in their relationships between schools and the homes of bilingual students. Next, I describe the context of this study within a semester-length course and with narrative inquiry as the chosen mode of research. Following this are excerpts from the family narratives, interpreted through the cultural roles framework. Finally, the implications of this project for educators, family participants, and researchers are addressed.

TEACHERS' CULTURAL ROLES

In educating minority language children and youth, teachers often serve as *cultural border guards*, inculcating the ways of the dominant culture while closing the door on students' own language and culture. How does this process work? First, there is often little contact between teachers and bilingual families (Valdes, 1996; Walker-Moffat, 1995). Problems being experienced by bilingual children are often blamed on "the home" (Delgado-Gaitan, 1996), and bilingual families are usually left out of conversations about second language education policies in the schools (Soto, 1997). The ways in which bilingual families and their children are perceived by teachers and schools are still greatly influenced by theories of cultural deprivation as an explanation of school failure.

Theories of cultural deprivation and a "culture of poverty," which emerged in the 1950s and 1960s, suggested that children from certain nondominant cultural groups grow up deficient in needed cultural attributes, and are trapped in a cycle of failure (Bereiter & Englemann, 1966; Lewis, 1966; McCandless, 1952). The implicit assumption behind cultural deprivation theory is that the home culture (and language) is the problem, and that to succeed students from such homes must be taught to perform in traditional mainstream ways. Even federal legislation of the era, such as the Bilingual Education Act (U.S. Congress, 1968), which ostensibly supported services to students in their home language, was compensatory in nature, focusing on the deficiencies of nonnative English speakers (Brisk, 1998).

Nevertheless, recent research suggests that bilingual families contribute in valuable ways to their children's learning. Moll, Velez-Ibañez, and Greenberg (1989) identified *funds of knowledge,* sources of skills and information for daily living, in their work within a working-class Mexican-American community. In projects that include teachers as researchers of their communities, these funds of knowledge from students' homes become resources available for curricular innovation and pedagogical change. In a variation of this approach, Andrade (1998) engaged bilingual children as ethnographers of their communities and their classrooms. Ethnographic and narrative research has revealed rich portraits of the skills, strengths, and values present within bilingual and bicultural families (Carger, 1996; Hones, 1999; Valdes, 1996).

Because many teachers and schools lack a strong connection to the lives and learning of bilingual and bicultural families, there are important reasons to involve preservice and in-service teachers in family-based projects. In describing the success of a family studies program in New Mexico for preservice teachers, Grinberg and Goldfarb (1998) argued that teachers must be sensitized to realities of children's worlds and become skilled in the bridging of the worlds of the home and the school. McCaleb (1998) highlighted the importance of preservice teacher involvement with diverse families to promote literacy, while Olmedo (1997) described ways in which family oral histories gathered by teachers can be woven into the social studies and history curriculum. Research with linguistically and culturally diverse families, therefore, has implications for teacher education, academic achievement, school–community relations and the development of a multicultural curriculum.

Clearly teachers have the potential to play a variety of cultural roles in the lives of linguistically diverse youth: the teacher can be a *storyteller,* a collector of stories, and an interpreter; the teacher can be a *healer* who can help students adjust to life in the dominant culture without stripping away their own cultural understandings; building upon these two previous roles the teacher can be a *cultural worker* who addresses issues of power in the classroom and in society (see Table 2.1).

RESEARCH PROJECT WITH IMMIGRANT AND REFUGEE FAMILIES

In our university ESL and bilingual education programs, we attempt to address the urgent need to build bridges between schools and various linguistic and cultural communities. We seek to prepare teachers

- who value linguistic and cultural diversity, and understand their multiple cultural roles as second language educators;
- who can critically assess themselves, their schools and their society;
- who have the ability to engage in real educational problem-solving with others;
- who can use participatory action and narrative research to reach out to minority language communities and build authentic curriculum and instruction; and
- who are producers of knowledge and creative members of professional communities.

Students in our program represent a growing demographic diversity in our region: Approximately 70% of the students are of European-American heritage, 20% are Asian American (predominantly Hmong), and 10% are

TABLE 2.1

Potential Cultural Roles for Teachers*

Cultural Storyteller	*Cultural Healer*	*Cultural Worker*
Biographer. Uses her own autobiography as a reflective tool for practice; encourages students to tell and learn from their own cultural life stories (Ayers, 1989; Goodson, 1992; Paley, 1995).	**Therapist**. Seeks ways to address multiple cultural conflicts faced by minority students/families; to ease the transition into the dominant culture without sacrificing meaningful aspects of students' own culture (G. Spindler & L. Spindler, 1994).	**Border Guard**. Transmits the meta-narrative of the dominant culture (in the dominant language); seeks to prepare students with the cultural literacy they need to function in American society (Bloom, 1987; Hirsch, 1988; Schlesinger, 1992).
Ethnographer. Collects, interprets, values and utilizes as part of the curriculum stories/ knowledge from variety of student cultures (Delgado-Gaitan & Trueba, 1991; Diaz Soto, 1997; Moll & Greenberg, 1990).	**Trainer**. Prepares students with literacy tools to be fluent in the language/culture of power, to adapt without necessarily assimilating (Delpit, 1987; Gee, 1990; Gibson, 1988).	**Border Crosser**. Critically engages with multiple cultural/linguistic communities; helps students develop their counternarratives to the dominant culture's meta-narrative; actively works to create diverse democratic communities inside and outside the classroom (Giroux, 1997).

*The boundaries between these role descriptions are hazy at best. For example, the *ethnographer* can also be seen as a cultural healer and/or a cultural worker, and the *border guard* is also a cultural storyteller.

Hispanic (of diverse Latin-American origins). Most have grown up in one of the nearby communities, although some spent their early years in Thai refugee camps, The Philippines, Puerto Rico, and other diverse localities. In general, our students are hard working, they are interested in learning about other languages and cultures, and they have good academic preparation. What our students need, especially those coming from European American backgrounds, is a stronger connection to the lives of bilingual students and families in their homes and communities.

One of the courses in our licensure sequence, Principles of Bilingual/Bicultural Education, was chosen as a place to engage students in research with immigrant and refugee families. This course introduces students to broader sociology, politics, and policies of language and culture; it explores ethnographic and narrative tools available for doing research within minority language communities found in texts such as Valdes' (1996) *Con Respeto* and Walker-Moffat's (1995) *The Other Side of the Asian-American Success Story* and engages students in dialogues with members of bilingual families through a semester-length research project. The culmination of the bilingual family research projects are written family narratives from which students present excerpts as performance events. These narratives, co-authored and co-edited wherever possible with family members, document the stories of the participants, framed by the historical, cultural and sociological contexts of their lives as immigrants and refugees.

The dialogic teacher research project encourages participation of bilingual family members in the retelling of their own "stories" and voicing their ideas about issues of education inside and outside of schools (Lincoln, 1993). Teachers, as cultural border crossers, are expected to gain a deeper understanding of the lives and concerns of bilingual families, and to take a critical stance in support of these families and their *counternarratives*, or stories that provide a counterpoint to the dominant culture's depiction of minority groups (Giroux, 1997). There is also a need to inform the wider monolingual community about issues facing bilingual families and children.

Narrative research is valuable mode of inquiry for this dialogic research process. Denzin's (1994) *interpretive interactionism*, involving the organization of life histories around "epiphanies" or life-shaping events, has been particularly influential for student researchers. This style "begins and ends with the biography and the self of the researcher," and encourages personal stories that are thickly contextualized, and "connected to larger institutional, group and cultural contexts" (pp. 510–511). Moreover, the stories presented in the text "should be given in the language, feelings, emotions, and actions of those studied" (p. 511). As indicated in the work of Grumet (1991) and McBeth and Horne (1996), many ethical and methodological issues need to be addressed in the writing of bilingual/bicultural narratives, especially when not all student researchers share the same cultural background as their informants. The importance of addressing the informants stories in a respectful manner is underscored, and family research participants are included in the process of analysis, interpretation, and, wherever possible, as co-authors of the final text.

In the opening weeks of class, students write autobiographically of their own connections to language, culture, family and education. They are asked to keep their personal stories in mind as they embark on narrative, ethnographic research with volunteering minority language families over a 10-week period. Individuals and small groups of students are paired with each family, learning about their lives and initiating dialogues about the education of their children. Thus, data sources for this research include, with permission from students and their informants, students' written accounts of their own lives, transcriptions of audiotaped interviews with research participants, field notes, videotapes and photographs of family life and library research.

NARRATIVES AND THE RENEGOTIATION
OF BOUNDARIES

One of the products of the dialogic teacher research project are written narratives of family lives. These narratives highlight the multiple voices of participants involved in the research, including the voices and autobiographical experiences of the researchers themselves. Moreover, these narratives served to illustrate the cultural roles as storytellers, healers, and workers that pre- and in-service teachers fulfilled as part of this project. Excerpts from these narratives illustrate the journey undertaken by these students of bilingual family lives, and what they have learned about how to bridge the two worlds of school and home.

Students awareness of the importance of their "biographer" role increased after writing their own cultural autobiographies. One of our students, a third-generation Polish American, writes of her search for information about her family cultural heritage:

> When I decided to get to know my own roots, there weren't very many people left who knew the stories behind the immigration of my great-grandparents. It seemed as if Judga and Busia never shared stories about their homeland, their village, their reason for leaving all that was familiar to them behind. Instead, I had to find my stories in courthouses, archives, and family history centers. (Kiedrowski, 1998)

With their appreciation of their own cultural past comes a new interest in creating opportunities for their minority language students to retell their life experiences with language and culture. Several of our students develop curricular units that integrate language skills and content areas by using storytelling as a theme. For example, one of our in-service teachers, with the support of a Hmong community activist, prepared her elementary ESL students to dramatically present stories of the Hmong people. The children helped choose stories to enact, developed and practiced their individual characters, their dialogues and scenes, and with the help of the teacher, parents and the community activist, organized their stage costumes, set, and props. The final dramatic presentation of these stories, in English and Hmong, was given to their entire elementary school and invited guests.

Our students often see a clear connection between their roles as storytellers and healers. While engaging in ethnographic interviewing with a Hmong parent, one of our students also played the role of the therapist by acknowledging both her informant's traumatic cultural struggle as well as her culture's strength:

> Mee said, "The most difficult thing about my life was when my mom, my brothers and my own two children died and my husband leaving me. I was left alone not knowing how to do anything ... I am waiting to die ..."

> My heart hurt for her as I watched her cry ... I asked her if she wanted me to stop interviewing her and shut off the tape recorder. She shook her head ... Mee has great inner strength to have gone this far ... I truly believe that what has made Mee strong mentally has been the strong Hmong tradition of self-reliance and independence. Her children and other Hmong people living close to her have given her support and other opportunities to help her survival in the United States. (Thompson, 1998)

Children of immigrants often grow apart from their parents as they adapt more quickly to the new language and culture, and as they lose the ability to really communicate across generations. One of the goals of the family narrative project (to be described) was to provide a forum in which the stories of parents and other elders could be explicitly valued by teacher-researchers, and to initiate a process of cultural therapy (G. Spindler & L. Spindler, 1994) between generations.

The family narratives reflect the emerging dialogue between the student-researchers and their informants. Through family interviews our students became aware of the tremendous importance that minority parents place on education. Often these parents have limited English skills and little formal education, yet they find ways to support their children's learning, as in the case of Xia, a Hmong mother:

> The only formal education Xia had were the two years of adult school when she arrived in America. Because Xia lacks skills in English, her husband, who

understands English better, attends the teacher–parent conferences. However, in supporting the children in other school related functions such as school awards night, movie nights, etc., it is Xia who attends with the children. Even though Xia is unable to carry on a full conversation in English, she is courageous and unintimidated by unknown situations. (Vang, Robinson, & Smith, 1998)

Students reflected on our earlier discussion of the ethnocentric attitudes and values often present in parent education programs (Valdes, 1996) and were able to use these family narrative studies to begin to identify culturally sensitive ways to encourage families to support the educational experiences of their children.

Personal stories shared by participating families about life and death on the United States–Mexican border stand in stark contrast to the political furor over illegal immigration that has garnered so much media and policy attention. One of the Mexican mothers interviewed had to cross the border at Nogales separated from one of her children. From a McDonald's restaurant window she watched her youngest child taken back across the border three times by *la migra*, the border patrol:

Four times she had to cross. She had the figure of a little saint in her hand. It gave me goose bumps. I felt very bad because she told me later, "Look, mommy! This helped me cross." I felt better with my older girls, but I also felt bad because I saw that they were so strong. They didn't cry. They didn't yell, nothing. I was happy that they didn't cry, but sometimes I feel bad because they were so young. (Lupe, interviewed in Serrano, Dryer, Fink, & Cortes, 1998)

Although they are supportive of the cultural worker roles, some students, especially those who work with Latinos, take issue with the *border guard* descriptor, and have suggested the term *gatekeeper* instead. Nevertheless, it becomes clear to our students that whichever term was chosen, there is the implication that one culture, one language, and one grand or meta-narrative are seen as important: Students either assimilate to these, or they are shut out. On the other hand, the *border crosser* seeks to prepare students with the tools necessary to be heard in the dominant language and culture, and moreover to use these tools to develop *counternarratives*—stories of their lives and communities that offer critical perspectives to those of the dominant culture. Students came to appreciate their own need to become cultural border crossers by listening to the real border crossing experiences of families.

Students, sometimes accompanied by their participant co-authors, have arranged to present this family narrative research at in-services in their school districts, at community service organizations, and at professional conferences. The written narratives are disseminated through journals and edited volumes as well. This dialogic teacher research project provides a forum for bilingual family members to share their stories and ideas, and for preservice and in-service teachers to learn from the families they serve and to begin making contributions to the field of second language practice and research.

Story Weaving: Critical Questions for Dialogic Researchers

With each day in New York, with each new session attended at the international TESOL conference, Chan and Khou Lor, refugees from Laos, became more animated as they discussed ideas for the future: He wants to attend the conference next year, in Vancouver; he wants me to come back with him to Laos to help document some of the stories of the forested highlands; he wants to go to the university, and get a degree in educational counseling, while his wife, Khou, appears ready to pursue licensure as a bilingual teacher. Along with Faye Van Damme, they also see themselves as writers of lives whose work will be of interest to others. After meeting with editors one evening, we return to find that firemen have converged on our cheap, midtown Manhattan hotel to answer a false alarm. Khou makes sure to get some photographs, "for the book."

Like the Lors, other participants in the dialogic teacher research project appear to benefit greatly from the bilingual family research project. In order to improve the research process and provide guidance for other researchers, family and student participants have identified several questions to consider:

How Do We Build Rapport and Trust?   Time is an important factor in establishing a trusting relationship with all participants in ethnographic and narrative research. Paradoxically, we were attempting to carry out a narrative research project over the period of a university course, a period of a few months. This posed special problems for students who had no prior familiarity with the families they were researching. In-service teachers who worked with the families of their students, on the other hand, found it much easier to begin their studies with some prior rapport already established. Nevertheless, students who made the effort to do utilize additional research on the cultural backgrounds of their participating families proved successful in establishing a relationship. One of the techniques we suggested to all students was to bring home country maps and other relevant cultural artifacts to their initial meetings with participating families, and this served to raise the level of interest and involvement in the study on the part of participants. Also, it was clear that sensitivity when conversing and asking questions, as well as a relaxed, personable approach served students well. Participating family members were able to see them as people, different than, but also similar, to themselves, and sharing a common concern with the effective education of all young people.

How Do We Gather and Arrange Stories? Problems frequently mentioned by students gathering stories involved finding ways to overcome language barriers and challenges with the interview environment and equipment. Although there were definitely issues of important details being lost in translation, for the most part, our students found ways to communicate effectively with at least some of the members of the bilingual families. Many of our students were able to use their Spanish-speaking skills when interviewing immigrant families from Mexico. Some of our native Hmong-speaking students worked collaboratively with other students to interview Hmong families in creative ways: the Hmong-speaking students would interview those in the family, such as the parents, who were less fluent in English, while the non-Hmong speaking students would interview older children who could communicate quite well in English. It was generally felt that the homes of the bilingual families offered the ideal interview sites, as the participants felt most comfortable there. However, as these natural settings included the sounds of children playing, radio music, and dinner being prepared, there was some interference on tape recordings of interviews. Nevertheless, students were able to use these additional sounds to recapture the spirit of such homes, where life, in all its vitality, goes on.

Once stories were gathered and transcribed, students and family participants were faced with decisions on how best to arrange these stories into a narrative. Interestingly, many chose to focus on life-changing events, what Denzin (1994) referred to as *epiphanies.* For many, it was a border crossing experience. For others, important events included births and deaths, interactions with employers or the schools, and even dreams.

How Do We Represent and Interpret the Stories Shared? Students also addressed the ethical implications of how to represent the stories of these bilingual families. Most chose to represent larger sections of participant voices in the text, and to show moods and feelings through their careful physical descriptions of the participants and their world. Many of our students, following the lead of Tedlock (1983), Richardson (1992) and others, chose poetry as a form well-suited to suggest the emotive power of participant voices. When drafts of initial texts were shared with family members, participants were able to clarify and extend their ideas, as well as approve or suggest changes to the forms in which their stories were represented. Wherever possible, students were able to produce, and share bilingual texts with participating families. For family members who had low literacy levels, our students were asked to represent, and request participant comments, orally, in a language understood by those involved.

Who Benefits From This Research, and How?   Our students gained a depth of understanding and sensitivity to students and their families, as well as knowledge of diverse cultures and ongoing cultural change. In-service teachers involved in the project have said that it has improved their ability to communicate effectively with all the families of their students. Some have taken the written record of immigrant and refugee stories and experiences and begun to weave it into their social studies and language arts curriculums. Many of our students remain in contact with the families they interviewed, continuing to learn from them, and sharing their talents with family members as tutors in English and other academic subjects.

Family participants, especially parents, feel that this project has helped them to preserve the history of their people and their family history for their children. Moreover, they have had the opportunity to inform the mainstream population about why they are here in the United States, what their lives are about, and the strengths of their cultures.

Educational research can benefit from projects that connect teacher education to bilingual and bicultural families and homes. Participative narrative research broadens our understanding of learning as it takes place within immigrant families, of ways in which teachers develop their various cultural roles, and how entire schools and communities can learn from the sharing of these stories. Sharing of personal and cultural stories is at the heart of work of building bridges between diverse groups of Americans who are divided all too often by ignorance and stereotypes.

At a time when bilingual education in the United States is under attack, family-based research can provide opportunities for teachers-as-researchers to better understand the socio-cultural and historical contexts, the learning processes, and the needs of minority language families. Moreover, by establishing a research relationship based on trust and respect, by creating space for bilingual family members to develop and tell their counter-narratives to the dominant culture (Giroux, 1997), teachers-as-researchers can become better allies and advocates for a meaningful system of bilingual/bicultural education.

Family-based research experiences, as an integral part of a teacher education program, help engage students in problem-posing education, encourage students to think of themselves as writers and researchers, and initiate greater dialogue between families, communities, schools, and the academy. We all have important cultural roles to play in fostering a climate where diverse stories and interpretations of our lives together can be shared.

FOUR DIALOGIC TEACHER RESEARCH NARRATIVES

In the section that follows, four dialogic teacher research projects with refugee and immigrant families are highlighted. The Hmong, Mexican, Assyrian, and Kosovar families chosen are representative of the bilingual and bicultural demographics that are changing our regional schools and communities. Maps and cultural group historical, political, and cultural profiles help to establish a context, but the heart of each chapter is a family narrative. The teacher researchers who wrote these chapters are representative of our program and the challenge we have of meeting the needs of immigrant and refugee families. Four of the five researchers— Faye Van Damme, Judy Mehn, Katie Hinz, and Jessica Wade-Martinez— are European Americans who have spent most of their lives in Wisconsin. The fifth, Maya Song-Goede, is a Hmong American who moved to Wisconsin as a child. None of the researchers could rely on extensive insider cultural knowledge or bilingual abilities during their interviews. The challenge they faced in this research mirrors the challenge faced by the majority of European-American teachers working with bilingual and bicultural children and families. They met this challenge by sharing of themselves and their stories, investigating the political, historical, and cultural backgrounds of their participating families, and engaging with family members with open minds and hearts.

II
Family Narratives

3

A Hmong Family

REFUGEES FROM LAOS

The history of the Hmong people can be traced back at least 5,000 years. Over time, the Hmong have wandered, or been driven, southward through China, from the fertile river valleys to the harsher environment of the high mountains. Centuries of struggle with the Chinese empire climaxed in the so-called "Miao" Rebellion in Guizhou Province from the 1850s to the 1870s. The rebellion ended with a province destroyed, millions reported dead, and the Hmong people serving as scapegoats for the wider peasant revolt against high taxes and the injustices of the central government. To preserve their lives and their freedom, many Hmong moved southward, into Vietnam, Laos, Thailand, and Burma (Jencks, 1994). In a brief overview to the Hmong's long history of struggle and relocation, Trueba and Zou (1994) asked: "What would make us think that the (Hmong)—after centuries of migration—have retained an ethnic identity, a sense of peoplehood?" (p. 3).

In 1959, the CIA, concerned about the growing communist insurgencies in Southeast Asia, began seeking the support of the Hmong of Laos.[1] The Hmong under the leadership of General Vang Pao agreed to provide military support and to help build air bases for the Americans near their villages. By the early 1960s the Americans and the Russians were heavily arming the opposing factions within Laos, and war engulfed the Hmong people in the

---

[1]There is evidence that the Americans became involved in opium trafficking in Southeast Asia, and that Long Chieng base served as a collection site for heroin processing. McCoy (1991) documented Vang Pao's involvement in the trade, including his establishment of a heroin lab at Long Chieng and the use of American helicopters to bring harvested opium into the base from outlying villages.

The Hmong in Laos

north. As is usual in war, the first casualty was the truth: Most Americans were not told of the U.S. involvement in Laos until 1970. What the Hmong were told was that the American's would come to their aid should the war go badly. The Hmong under the leadership of Vang Pao agreed to fight with the Americans against communists in Southeast Asia. A decade and more of the "secret war" in Laos left thousands of Hmong dead and dozens of villages destroyed, especially in Xieng Khouang Province on the border with Vietnam (Hamilton-Merritt, 1993).

In 1973, the Paris Peace Accords signaled the end of American military involvement in Southeast Asia; in Laos, a peace agreement was signed between the warring factions. Two years later, the Pathet Lao communists pressured the Laotian king to send Vang Pao out of the country. As the Vietnam War came to an end, the North Vietnamese Army and Pathet Lao closed in on Hmong strongholds in the north of Laos. Vang Pao and several of his supporters were airlifted out of the airbase at Long Chieng, but thousands of Hmong men, women and children were left behind to fend for themselves, no longer with American support. Many died in a war of attrition carried out by the new Lao People's Democratic Republic and their Vietnamese allies (Hamilton-Merritt, 1993). Moreover, much of the high mountain agricultural system had been destroyed in the war, and the Hmong faced an economically bleak future (Cooper, 1986).

With the proclamation of the Lao People's Democratic Republic in 1975, many changes came to the Hmong villages. Old village leaders were replaced with new. Small private farms were consolidated and collectivized. Traditional gender, family, and communal relationships were challenged. Free public education was extended to the remotest mountain villages. "Seminars" were arranged for those who were unable or unwilling to adapt to the new changes, and many never returned from their stays in the reeducation camps (Hamilton-Merritt, 1993). A vast exodus occurred as Vang Pao's soldiers and their families, Hmong clan leaders, and all those who were either unwilling or unable to live under communist rule left Laos for Thailand. The road was often treacherous, and encounters with communist troops could prove disastrous. The crossing of the Mekong is the theme of countless Hmong pandau, or story cloths, which depict vivid scenes of this part of Hmong history.

By the late 1970s, the eastern Thai border was home to 21 refugee camps set up to receive hundreds of thousands of people fleeing Vietnam, Cambodia, and Laos. These camps were supported by the United Nations High Commissioner for Refugees (UNHCR) and staffed by volunteers, among whom were many missionaries. However, the Thai government was influential in determining official and unofficial refugee camp policies. Camps were opened and closed by Thai authorities, and refugees were shifted about. In general, the Thais favored repatriation of refugees, even though many feared for their lives if they were returned to their homelands. "These periodic shifts from camp to camp effectively terrorized the refugees, because they could never be certain when they would be uprooted again or, worse yet, sent across the border" (Long, 1993, p. 49; see also The Lawyers Committee for Human Rights, 1989).

Tens of thousands of Hmong were living in camps in Thailand by 1980, principally in Chiang Kham, Ban Nam Yao, and the large camp at Ban Vinai. Ban Vinai, the largest Hmong settlement in the world at that time, contained over 40,000 people in an area of less than 1 square mile (Long, 1993). The reeducation of refugees destined for America began in these camps in Thailand. Tollefson (1989) suggested that refugees were presented with an unrealistic portrait of life in the United States, while at the same time, they were made to feel the unworthiness of their own cultures:

> The counterfeit universe presented to refugees in the educational program at the processing centers is planned and purposeful. The unrealistic vision of life in the United States, the myths of American success ideology, the denigration of Southeast Asian cultures, and the effort to change refugees' behavior, attitudes, and values result from systematic decisions by policymakers throughout the educational bureaucracy. (p. 87)

Camp life was squalid, crowded, and dangerous for refugees who feared reprisals from Lao communists, Thai communists, and Thai government soldiers. Despite the difficulties of the camps, however, many Hmong refugees did not want to "board the bus" for America (Ranard, 1989). The lessons of American success they learned in the reeducation programs were more than counterbalanced when they received letters from relatives in America, and read their tales of isolation, poverty, and fear in strange cities.

The first Hmong refugees arrived in Fox Valley, Wisconsin, in 1975, and today they make up the largest minority group in the area. In the following pages, Faye Van Damme, a preschool ESL teacher who works mostly with Hmong children, presents her dialogic teacher research with the Lor family. Assisted by her bilingual paraprofessional, Khou Lor, Ms. Van Damme focuses on the life of Chan Lor, orphaned at an early age in Laos, and now adjusting to life in the United States.

FIG. 3.1. Khou and Chan Lor at the United Nations Building,
New York City, March 1999.

FIG. 3.2. Khou and Chan Lor with Faye Van Damme,
New York City, March 1999.

— THE LORS —

Faye A. Van Damme With Chan and Khou Lor

January 15, 1983. The misty air hung heavy around the jungle covered mountains; hills of shelter and protection, as well as doom and death. This is a place with a war-ravaged countryside, where the inhabitants are homeless and hungry, where innocent farmers are prisoners, where one, young, 13-year old is without a father and mother, where darkness is all around.

January 15, 1983. The subzero temperatures grip the air sending chilly shivers down spines. The small town is encased in the white of midwinter snows. This is a place with a sense of comfort and security, where homeowners raise families and prosper, where streetlights illuminate the roadways leading to supermarkets and schools, where citizens live freely, where one, young, 17-year-old is surrounded by family and friends, where darkness is all around.

The darkness is broken by bursts of light: one by gunfire and land mines; the other by birthday candles and flashbulbs. In the days prior to this date, preparations have been made for each of the events occurring half a globe apart. Secret meetings were held in the safety of the trees, messages were carried on the lips of the couriers, escorts and boats were arranged, money was spent. Guest lists were written and invitations mailed, messages sealed in colorful envelopes, decorations and games were arranged, money was spent.

As the day approaches and the events unfold, emotions are intensified by anticipation. For the Hmong boy of Laos, there is tension, eagerness, nervousness, danger, and urgency, as he prepares to leave his mother behind in the hilltops to cross the mighty Mekong with his uncle's family. For the Anglo girl of Wisconsin, there is excitement, eagerness, lightness, gaiety, and high spirits as she awaits the arrival of guests.

There is much laughter and frivolity as friends and family enter the balloon- and streamer-filled house. Games are played, gifts are opened, and cake is eaten, all in the name of fun.

There is no laughter, only seriousness and dead quiet. It is a 15-mile walk to the shores of safety. It is unknown who is going to die. Many lose their feet from walking on land mines. Shirttails are held, boats are loaded, and strangers are trusted, all in the name of freedom.

January 15, 1983. On this day two people, separated by land and sea, experience two totally contrasting events. On this day one experiences a celebration of birth, while one experiences a celebration of rebirth.

How is it possible that two people from unlike cultures with extremely different pasts should happen to meet in Oshkosh, Wisconsin? Currently, I am teaching preschool English as a Second Language (ESL). Because the class is composed of Hmong students, I have a bilingual assistant who is Hmong. Over the course of the school year, we have established a relationship that reaches beyond a professional one; we have built a friendship. When I first learned of this family narrative study, I immediately thought of telling the story of my assistant, Khou. After explaining the project to her, she responded, "My story isn't very interesting, you should talk to my husband, Chan." And so it was decided that I would tell the story of Chan Lor. The following pages hold the history, thoughts, and feelings of Chan as he grew up in Laos, fled, relocated to the United States, and was "educated" in American schools and society. I have a special interest in the role school played in Chan's life, as well as his thoughts and viewpoints of the responsibilities schools have to immigrants.

Chan Lor's Story

Not so long ago, a boy child was born. I am that first born child. My name is Chan Lor, and I was born in the small, mountain village of Xieng Khouang, Laos, in 1970. At that time, my dad was a CIA agent who had joined the Hmong army at age 11. When I was 1 year old, my family and I moved to the large modern city of Long Cheng. The airport was busy and cars filled the streets. This is where the American CIA headquarters were located. Even before the CIA arrived, Long Cheng was a city, compared to most of Laos, where agrarian villages dotted the lush mountainsides.

Due to the war with the communists, we moved a lot as I was growing up. In 1973, my dad died. No one is quite sure what happened to him. He was just missing. Since he was a soldier fighting against the communists, it is most likely he was killed. My mom and I went to live with my mom's parents when I was 5 years old. We made the journey from Long Cheng to my grandparents' mountain village by foot, as was the customary mode of travel.

Here we stayed for about 1 year. When the communists invaded, many people panicked. In 1976, my grandparents, my mom, and I walked to the village of Pusongoi, where we thought we would be safe. Later that year, we fought communists who burned houses and were shooting in Pusongoi. We walked for 2 or 3 weeks to reach Mong Au. As we crossed to Mong Au, family members were protected by the villagers. Muong Cha, a city the size of Oshkosh, is close to Mong Au, where my mother is now living. Mong Au is close to the big city, but takes 1 day to walk. My mom remarried in 1978.

In 1980, the communists came again, shooting. At that time, every village in Laos was controlled by the communists, and we could not stay there; we just kept moving. The villagers moved to the jungle. In the jungle, there was no food, no rice, no anything. I was 10 years old and have strong memories of this time. We stayed hidden under the trees and banana leaves. The quiet and not knowing what was going to happen was scary.

We ate something like a potato which we dug out of the ground with a knife. We also caught animals in something like a snare. We could only cook on cloudy days so that the smoke from the fires would not be discovered. There was no salt for cooking. At that time the salt was so expensive. You could buy an amount of salt the size of a quarter for 1 ghee, which was worth about $12. We could stay in one place in the jungle for about 1 week before all the food was gone. Before moving on, we would have to put everything back (ground cover) so as not to reveal our presence to the communists. We had to move because if we didn't, they would know the place where we were living.

They (communists) used low airplanes to locate us. If they saw smoke, they would shoot on the ground. The soldiers in the planes would call the soldiers on the ground by radio. They would shoot very large guns that could shoot from here (Oshkosh) to Green Bay, about 60 miles. Lots of children died because parents drugged them to keep them quiet or they were shot by soldiers who found the children crying. This was such a terrible time. Parents even left their children in the jungle.

After 6 months of living in the jungle, we could not handle it, so we went back to Mong Au. My mother and stepfather stayed in Mong Au. My uncle (father's brother) took me with him and his family. We headed to the Mekong River.

The steep mountains, kind of like those in Colorado, were all around us as we started walking barefoot toward the Mekong. There were a lot of mountains, not like here. You climb one day; you climb one mountain. We walk twisting up the mountainside. It is like walking to the sky. You climb up like that, and when you get to the top, you go down. Because we didn't like the area in the valleys, we went in the mountains, so the communists didn't know where we were. The mountains were a big area the soldiers didn't control. The mountains were very, very big. In Laos, they have these vines like a string you can put around you, and you can pull a person high up and down. A lot of people, like 100, would be tied together. Sometimes the string would get cut. The people would be 100 yards high and fall.

The distance from Mong Au to the Mekong was about a 13- or 14-day walk, in ideal conditions, without children or provisions. The distance is not very long, but because we were walking in the mountains, carrying baskets of food and had children with us, it took almost 1 month to reach the river. We were traveling in a group of 500 people. We stopped near a big mountain close to Paksane and stayed there for 5 days.

Four Laotian men said they had a boat. They knew the way and told us to get our money together. It cost about $40 for each person. We collected the money, at which time the Laotian men told us to wait in the jungle while two of the Laotians went to rent the boat. We were told they would be back in 2 days. Two hundred more Hmong people came to join the group. After 5 days we see nothing. People were very hungry, as we had no food and were eating only leaves. At midnight, it was so dark, we were running. A group of 300 people went close to the Mekong. It was so dark, they could not see where they were going. Many Hmong people died here, because the soldiers heard the children crying and began shooting.

I was with a group of 400 people about a half mile away. We stayed hidden on a Laotian farm. We knew we could not run, we had no food, no anything. We knew we could not go back to the mountains; we would die. In the morning, we just surrendered with a little flag. We came out of the jungle and surrendered. There were soldiers in the area because they knew people had been trying to cross the river during the night.

We were taken to Paksane, a Laotian city near the Mekong River. I lived with my uncle, aunt, and two cousins here for the next 3 years. During that time, we were given rice, and we had homes and farms. No one owned the land in Laos at this time. Anyone who worked the land could have it. If you were there first, no one could touch the land. Daytime was spent fishing a lot. Evenings were spent telling stories, because no one could go anywhere. Stories about tigers were often told. In Laos, the tiger is the most ferocious monster, feared by everyone.

I went to school for 2 or 3 months. I learned how to read, write, and speak Laotian. I learned ABCs and math. Books were too expensive, so we used little chalkboards and chalk. We wrote everything the teacher wrote on the chalkboard. We had to memorize the material. If you made mistakes, rocks were put on the floor, and you had to kneel on the rocks with your arms out. You were hit by whoever could answer correctly. If you were doing the hitting, you had to hit as hard as you could or you would get hit. It was very embarrassing to be punished, especially by a girl. Students studied hard so that they would not shame their families or be embarrassed. There was a lot of pressure in this type of school environment. I was once hit because I did not study hard the night before.

I had an uncle living in Colorado. He paid Thai people to escort my family across the Mekong River. The arrangements were made secretively in the jungle or on the edges of farms. Messages were passed word of mouth to my uncle. The crossing was 15 miles from Paksane during the night. On the walk to the Mekong, we did not know who was going to die. A lot of people lost their feet from walking on landmines. A lot of people died swimming across the river. Soldiers out in boats would spear the people with knives or shoot them with guns. We were fortunate to cross by boat. In the night, we stayed close to each other and held on to each other's shirt. My aunt and uncle became my parents, but I missed my mother very much because I was still so young at this time. To stay in Laos was terrible. It didn't matter how dangerous the crossing was, we just wanted to cross. Crossing would lead to happy times. On January 15, 1983, that is just what we did; my family crossed the Mekong River to the safety and freedom of Thailand.

For 1 month we stayed in a refugee camp called Nong Khai. Here we had to have a letter written which included our name, birth date, and other pertinent information. In Laos, my people did not keep track of birthdays the way you do in America. My uncle did not know when I was born, so he said I was born in 1973, the time my father died. While we were in Nong Khai, we were able to get food and rations for our family. We left Nong Khai and rode a bus to Ban Vinai, where we lived for a year. It was a terrible life living in the camps. We boarded the bus January 22, 1984. The stop at this camp would be the last stop before boarding the plane to the United States. We stayed here for 6 months learning English and preparing to leave Southeast Asia.

I had a very sad life. It is hard in the camps when you see some parents buying anything the children want. If I had parents I could have it, too. My life, at the time, living in Laos, was dark. I had to cross the Mekong River to get my new life because I didn't like to stay. I missed my mother, too. I had to make a new life, even as a child.

I was on the last leg of my journey to freedom. I entered the bus and was carried to the airport, where I boarded a plane and began the long ride to the United States. I had "grandparents" living in Oshkosh at that time, who sponsored my family to move to Oshkosh. Any older person is called a grandparent out of respect for the older person.

September 27, 1984, I arrived in Oshkosh. I was really 14 years old, but was considered 11 years old according to my papers. I was in the fifth grade at Washington School. There were only three Hmong students in the school at that time. Although my classmates were accepting of me, and the teachers were caring, I was so much bigger and older than the rest of the class. I felt like an outsider; I did not know the language. I was eager to learn, to learn the language. I was placed in a regular classroom, as there was no ESL instruction at this time. Overall, I had a positive school experience. I was free—meaning there was no one to watch everything I did or said. I could travel to other cities and states, and no one would ask questions like, "Why are you going to that city or state?" There was no permit or paperwork involved. I was making a new life.

The Dialogue: Faye Van Damme and Chan Lor (March 1998)

The second chapter of Chan's story is under way. A lot has happened since he arrived in 1984. He has attended the University, has a wife and two small boys, has a job, plays soccer, and maintains his Hmong language and traditions. The latter is strong and alive for Chan; unfortunately this is not true for all immigrants.

Many immigrants throughout the course of history have found it difficult, and in some cases impossible, to maintain their native language and traditions. In the United States, there has been a strong push for immigrants to assimilate, to be absorbed into the cultural tradition of a population or group. For immigrants, this has meant to become identical to or similar to White Americans. Shah (1994) shared his opinion of assimilation, which is likely to be an opinion shared by many:

> Assimilation assumes that there is one right culture. We [immigrants] want to maintain a separate identity and culture, so we can educate our young to not join a gang, to get a good education, to get jobs. When the government promotes cultural diversity, they are not serious about learning about other people's cultures. Their suggestion usually is "just read this book and you'll know everything about it." (p. 122)

When asked about his own assimilation into American culture, Chan responded:

> I feel I have assimilated about 75% to the American culture, because we need to obey all the laws and policies and understand right from wrong—but I need to keep my culture alive by not losing my language.

> There are no real difficulties that I experience, except that with me having my own culture and traditions. I see all the different cultures that are in the United States. It makes it a little difficult to understand why people hate one another when we are all human beings. We should be able to live together under one roof, but that is not the case because we [people in general] only like our own kind.

Why is it so difficult for people of different backgrounds to live together and be accepted? Why is it when almost everyone living in the United States has descended from immigrant ancestors, America continues to be a land of inequity with emphasis on individualism rather than on community responsibility?

How has this inequity effected our communities' Hmong population, whose culture is rooted in the strength of the family unit or clan, whereby the good of the clan is held to a higher level than the good of any individual member? How do the Hmong view themselves and how do they fit into

American society? What does it mean to be American Hmong? Lee (1996) felt being a Hmong in America is not the same as being an American Hmong or Hmong American: The first still keeps his culture and language, the second has lost them. He goes on to say, we need to fulfill our responsibilities as citizens of our respective countries of adoption, but we need to appreciate our "Hmongness."

Wanting to have a first-hand, personal view point of this, I asked Chan how he felt about Lee's comments. He replied:

> I agree that being a Hmong American, a person will lose his or her culture and language because he or she is too excited to be in America. He or she will try to do everything like an American, forgetting who he or she really is—like speaking only English and dying his or hair blonde or other colors. I see myself as a Hmong living in America, because even though I speak English at school and work, when I go home, I only speak Hmong. I try to teach Hmong beliefs and values to my children. I know how to read and write Hmong. I practice Hmong ceremonies, and I know how to sing Hmong folk songs, play the love flute, and enjoy taking to the elders about Hmong cultures and values. I have a dream of one day returning to my own country because I miss the surroundings and scenery.

I was intrigued by Chan's comment about wanting to return to Laos. I probed a bit more and found that despite his level of assimilation and relative comfort in living in the United States, he feels powerless because he is a minority. Chan speaks directly to the previously mentioned inequity in America. He does not feel he can be politically involved because of his ethnic background. He wants to participate actively in the community, but feels he has no say. He would like to have his own business, which would be much easier if he was living in Laos. For whom is America "the land of opportunity?" Shah (1994) suggested "We [Southeast Asians] have to be represented in every facet of this country, not assimilation, but full participation" (p. 124). Human societies have reached the stage where they now actively engage one another. This engagement has resulted in a world that consists increasingly of blended rather than discrete cultures, a cultural mesh or "pastiche," which mixes all styles and materials, borrows from all sources, and rejects traditionally accepted standards (Lee, 1996, p. 71).

Although nations are globally connected, minority populations continue to feel great despairs and devalued as humans. One Hmong women said, "If I could come back [in the next life], I would not want to be a Hmong. To be Hmong is to be very miserable, maybe if one were born into a different race, life would be better" (Mattison, Lo, & Scarseth, 1994). For this woman life has been very hard, whereby, she attributes her ethnicity as the cause of her hardships. Chan has responded to this woman's comments by saying:

I don't agree with this woman's response. She is Hmong. When she dies her body, soul, and spirit will be Hmong. She will be wearing her traditional costume when she dies. She cannot be reincarnated into another race. What she needs to do is to turn around and help the Hmong people by encouraging higher education for the younger population, so we as a race can better ourselves and live richer lives.

From his response, it is quite clear that Chan is deeply connected and guided by traditional Hmong beliefs. He has suggested education, rather than a different ethnicity, is the key to a better life.

As a society we can begin to educate our children within the schools, but before that will even be successful, teachers need to be made aware of their own cultural roles of storyteller, healer, and cultural worker. In many cases, teachers will need instruction and training in these roles. It seems impossible to empower students and diminish the inequity that exists if those directly involved in educating students are unaware of their responsibility. The responsibility lies with all teachers, not only with the ESL or bilingual teachers. If any meaningful learning, in relation to multiculturism, is to be passed from educators to students, the educators themselves must have an understanding and acceptance of the backgrounds the students bring with them. Chan believes that teachers need to understand that culture can affect a student's performance in school, so they [the students] need extra time to think and understand assignments that are given. Lee (1996) believed that the more we understand each other's cultures, the more we are likely to show mutual tolerance.

The task of educating minority students does not come in a simple, neat package. The larger society is mirrored in the structure and composition of public schools, which have become a futuristic microcosm of American society, and as such reflect the same biases and prejudicial attitudes toward minorities. School teachers and administrators are torn between the dilemma of American democratic ideals advocating educational opportunity for all, and the low expectations shared by most Americans of minority students' achievement (Trueba, Jacobs, & Kirton, 1990). The function of the schools is to socialize youth into American cultural values and prepare them to play a role in society, provide knowledge, and mainstream immigrant and minority students. Achievement is the expected outcome of teaching, learning, and the overall experience of schooling.

Teachers are not alone in the struggle of educating the immigrant children. Parents also feel frustration with the educational process. For many, the lack of personal experience with formal education limits the role the parents play in their child's education. Parents may not know or may be limited in their level of English; they may not know what to expect from American schools, how to be involved, or what questions to ask regarding the schooling their children are receiving. Many times what parents consider discipline at home is seen as abuse by teachers. Parents feel it is their responsibility to nurture and teach obedience to their children. In Laos, corporal punishment is common and accepted. Parents have a difficult time raising their children by American standards. Here, then, lies a perfect opportunity for teachers to assume the role of cultural healer. In order for this to be successful, parents and teachers need to dialogue; sharing perspectives, backgrounds, and concerns. By working together, being viewed as joint forces rather than opposing forces, parents and teachers can strengthen their bond, benefitting the children. Open communication will lead to increased understanding with greater potential for conflict resolution, thus placing the children in an easier position.

Immigrant and refugee students have the challenge of learning English, fitting into the mainstream population, and yet maintaining their first language and customs. This is no easy endeavor because mainstream culture oftentimes clash with traditional cultural values. For example, when I asked Chan if he felt American schools should be more strict, he said:

> In the United States there is a lot of freedom given to everyone, so when in school, students can wear whatever they like. In Laos, all students need to wear the same uniforms. There is only public school. In Laos, students respect their teachers, meaning, they don't talk back at the teachers.
>
> The policy at [American] schools makes it too easy for students to go to school. Student can choose to skip school, be suspended, then come back to school. In Laos, the policy is very strict that if a student skips school and is suspended, he or she can not come back to school.

Hmong families like the Lors place a high value on education and view education as the means to improve their social position and make a better life for themselves. Education has always been valued, even when living in Laos. This was so because of the limitations the Hmong people experienced. They saw the schooled Laotians having more opportunities than themselves. Unlike America, where public school is compulsory and free, in Laos the public schools are open to anyone who can afford to attend. This has historically limited the education of Hmong children, who were needed to help tend the crops or smaller children. Due to the financial expense, if any Hmong child was going to go to school, only one child from a family would go, most often a male child.

How do Hmong families feel about the education being provided for their children in our public schools? I have heard positive comments regarding the education being offered. Parents like that all the children can attend school for free. School is seen as an opportunity for students to better themselves and take care of themselves. Being in school benefits children because they can learn English. At home, in many families, they only speak Hmong. Chan Lor shared this with me:

> Children's education is always an issue at gatherings because we need to have an education to better ourselves and to compete for a better life and job. The Hmong have always loved education and learning, because they are a poor culture and we want to better ourselves. Schools need to educate students as well as the community to be sensitive to different cultures. Cultures are not weird, they are just different.

For my friends, the Lors, it is quite clear education will continue to be a significant avenue for achievement, success, and prosperity. They, like many other families, see the importance of learning English and adapting to life as Americans. For Chan and his family, this means adapting as Hmong in America in order that the Hmong language and traditions will remain alive and an integral part of who they are. Chan's existence is rooted in tradition:

> Deep inside me I still know who I really am and where I came from. As a parent, I help preserve my culture by speaking Hmong at home to my kids, telling stories of Hmong heroes and folk tales, keeping Hmong tapestries and embroideries, and practicing Hmong ceremonies like the Basi and shaman ceremonies.

The goal of educators is to learn about the backgrounds of our students, promoting cultural diversity and acceptance. It may mean going beyond the walls of our own classrooms to expose our colleagues to the beauty of each individual child. It may also mean tapping into the community to share the stories of our immigrant families. If we are part of a knowledgeable, caring community, the possibilities are endless for all the people of the community. Each person's uniqueness can be seen as a resource not to be wasted away by prejudice and ignorance. You can be assured that Chan's story will continue to unfold as he lives and shares his traditions with his children. By sharing his personal story with me, and you, the reader, Chan has become an ambassador of tolerance and acceptance, but most importantly of humanness:

> We cannot achieve unity until we look at our shortcomings, broaden our minds by listening more to other people, by becoming tolerant, assertive, knowing how to speak and act without hurting people. When this is done we will be able to join hands and achieve the freedom we yearn for: freedom from poverty and ignorance, freedom to learn and progress, freedom to get together and to share, freedom from exploitation and from contempt. (Lee, 1986, p. 73)

Postscript

This dialogic research project has opened my eyes, challenged my abilities, and pushed me to question and explore my personal history. Throughout the journey of this project, beginning with the first interview with Chan to our trip to the TESOL conference in New York City, to the finishing stages in preparation for publication, the relationship that has developed has impacted me and my teaching. I have looked more closely at family relationships, the importance of home and school connections, and ways to share what I have learned with the larger community.

I am continually amazed by the close ties and the depth of extended family connections in the Hmong community. The Hmong are naturally connected via clan names; however, from my experience, extended family reaches far past the clan. There are many family gatherings in which all ages from infants to the elderly participate. These gatherings include, but are not limited to, birth ceremonies, weddings, New Year celebrations, spiritual healing ceremonies, funerals, camping trips, and family meetings. Families are often located closely together in the same or neighboring communities.

This is quite a contrast to many mainstream American families. Often nuclear families are small with one or two children. Families can be long distances from relatives, leading to limited, if any, regular contact with extended family, resulting in fewer family gatherings. My immediate family is a prime example. With my sister's family living in Indiana, my brother's family in Illinois, and my parents in northern Wisconsin, we are seldom able to gather together. Jobs and vacation time have also impacted the amount of time we are able to spend together. Ties with cousins, aunts, and uncles have weakened due to physical distance, demands of jobs, and lifestyle choices.

The history of one's family is invaluable. It impacts *who* we are, providing us with a foundation for who we are to become. In knowing our personal history, we, as educators, are better able to serve our immigrant students. It is through understanding ourselves that we have greater understanding of our students, their families, and their histories. Since listening to Chan tell his story of survival, escape, and family, I have begun making an effort to reconnect with my family. I have been spending more time with my only remaining grandparent to gather the stories of her past in order to have a better understanding of who my ancestors were.

This project has not only affected my personal life, but my professional life as well. I can see how valuable it is to establish a rapport with parents of students. This means reaching beyond the confines of the classroom and students. My current teaching position has time built into the schedule, which allows me to make home visits and meet with parents; during my visits, I am able to discuss concerns and successes students are having. At this same time, I am able to discover more about who the parents are and how this impacts the students.

Parent meetings in the classroom have been another avenue to gather information about the families I service. The meetings have become a forum in which I am able to offer parent workshops and programs from community agencies, and to listen to the concerns parents have regarding their children's education and the manner in which their children's needs are being met by our school district.

Over the past 4 years, I have worked with many of the same families. The parent relationships I have developed in one school year are only strengthened when I am able to teach other children in the same family. I feel I have built a trust with the families I work with and have developed friendships. I have been invited to New Year celebrations and weddings. These events that take place outside the classroom are rich with family tradition, native language, and culture, and provide a glimpse into my students' lives that I might have greater understanding of who they are.

Within my classroom instruction I have incorporated a family unit that celebrates each child's uniqueness. A class photo album includes pictures of students' families and pictures taken throughout the school year. Parents are invited to participate in a celebration day in which traditional foods are served, native games are played, and parents become teachers. Parents have shared artifacts, taught us origami, and have entertained us with oral storytelling.

Another aspect of professional responsibility is to reach out to the community and share what is happening in the classroom and/or who our immigrant families are. A local Kiwanis club teamed with our school; members of the club provided the students with gift bags at Christmas, chaperoned field trips, and read to the children. The children have also given to the adults. Even the youngest of children can make a lasting impression as one of the adult readers found out. One gentleman who had some negative feelings toward immigrant families had his mind and heart opened. I was able to share background information as to why the Hmong were living in Oshkosh and the children shared their innocence and enthusiasm for learning. After spending the year making weekly visits to our classroom, he had learned tolerance and acceptance of the immigrants in our community.

At the start of this school year, I implemented an intergenerational program with members of our local senior center. We have made monthly visits to the senior center to foster a relationship with older adults in our community. The monthly visits consist of a seasonal or theme-related project with time to talk and interact and book time with the adults reading to the children. The children look forward to seeing their senior friends; the program is growing in popularity with the seniors because each month their are more senior friends participating.

I believe our professional responsibility includes sharing projects, ideas, and experiences with colleagues and other professionals in the education field. Chan, Khou, Dr. Hones, and I were fortunate to have the opportunity to present Chan's story at a local conference and at the international TESOL conference in New York City 2 years ago.

The past 2 years have brought changes and growth for Chan and Khou. They have seen their family physically grow with the addition of another son. They have become U.S. citizens. Perhaps the most significant change has been Chan's dream of owning his own business and being his own boss. He and Khou opened an Asian food store in August 1999. Chan is happy making a comfortable living. He feels the long hours and hard work will be worth the effort in the long run.

Khou, on the other hand, feels differently. She feels the business is not as profitable as anticipated and includes more work than ever imagined. Juggling her responsibility as mother of three sons, her job outside the store, managing the home, fulfilling family obligations, and her duties at the store has been difficult. Khou does not think less time with her children, long hours, and less income than anticipated is worth the energy.

Despite their differing view points, Chan and Khou are working together to make their dream a success. Chan still has a strong interest in one day having a business in Laos, which would allow him to once again live in his native land.

FIG. 3.3.   Mai Vue Thao and her four daughters on Hmong New Year, 2000,
Oshkosh, Wisconsin.

FIG. 3.4.   Hmong New
Year, 2000, Oshkosh,
Wisconsin.

HMONG NEW YEAR

"You look so handsome!" says Mai Vue, smiling up at me as she cradles her 3-month-old child in her arms.

"Thanks," I replied. I did feel like a different man. Perhaps it was the tiny silver coins that jingled when I walked, or the comfortable feeling of the black, baggy pants. Perhaps it was something I saw in the eyes of the grandmothers who smiled as I walked by, or the quizzical looks cast by the teenagers I recognized from the high school. It was my fourth Hmong New Year at the Expo Center in Oshkosh, but my first time wearing traditional Hmong clothing.

Mai Vue had asked my wife if we would wear the Hmong clothes a few weeks before when she had stopped by our house. A few days before the New Year, we went over for a fitting. It takes time and help for the uninitiated to get dressed in Hmong clothing: First, I put on the black silky pants. Next, Neng, Mai Vue's husband, helped wrap several yards of pink cloth about my waist, and adjusted the brightly colored vest of silver coins. Then there were five hanging coin pockets that were tied at strategic points around my waistline. The beautiful, silver ornamented collar would not fit over my head, which was fortunate, as my wife wore one, and she reported that it was quite heavy. Underneath the vest of coins I was instructed to wear a white shirt and a tie.

We saw many friends at the New Year. Mr. Vang, my Hmong teacher, was master of ceremonies, and his daughter was there writing a story for the local newspaper. There were a number of teachers, bilingual assistants, and students from the public schools, many dressed in traditional clothing, and some playing the ball-tossing game. Khou and Chan Lor were there, preparing and selling traditional Hmong food. I was glad to notice many more non-Hmong participants in the gathering than I had seen in years past. As usual, the outsiders to Hmong culture are treated as special guests, and given seats of honor, and food, at a table near the mainstage.

The New Year performances afford a window into the ongoing cultural changes in Hmong America. There are traditional *qeng* players, and *a capella* singers intoning songs from Laos; there are traditional dances performed in both Hmong and Western dress; and there are boys in baggy pants and overcoats providing Hmong language counterpoints to the *Backstreet Boys*. One cannot fail to observe the contrast in styles between the old ways and the new, and yet there is a solidarity in this community that is palpable, that connects generations together like a melody played on different instruments. I always feel welcome here, no more so than this year, when I am honored to wear Hmong clothing.

Can we extend this sense of welcome to all those who stand on the outskirts of American life? Can we erase the lines of color, language and ethnicity that separate us, that prevent us from enjoying the fruits of a living, changing culture? As I sit here in the Expo Center listening to a rap song in a language I can't yet understand, I say that we can, and we will.

Nyob Zoo Xyoo Tshiab.

Happy New Year!

HMONG REFUGEES:
SUGGESTED READINGS AND WEB SITES

Chan, S. (Ed.). (1994). *Hmong means free: Life in Laos and America*. Philadelphia: Temple University Press.

Cheung, S. (1995). Millenarianism, Christian movements, and ethnic change among the Miao in Southwest China. In W. Harrell (Ed.), *Cultural encounters on China's ethnic frontiers* (pp. 217–247). Seattle: University of Washington Press.

Conquergood, D. (1989). *I am a Shaman: A Hmong life story with ethnographic commentary* (Occasional Paper No. 8). Minneapolis: University of Minnesota, Southeast Asian Refugee Studies Project.

Donnelly, N. (1994). *Changing lives of refugee Hmong women*. Seattle: University of Washington Press.

Dunnigan, T. (1986). Processes of identity maintenance in Hmong society. In G. Hendricks, B. Downing, & A. Deinard (Eds.), *The Hmong in transition* (pp. 41–54). New York: The Center for Migration Studies.

Fadiman, A. (1997). *The spirit catches you and you fall down: A Hmong child, her American doctors, and the collision of two cultures*. New York: Noonday Press.

Hmong Youth Cultural Awareness Project. (1994). *A free people: Our stories, our voices, our dreams*. Minneapolis, MN: Hmong youth cultural awareness project.

Hones, D., & Cha, S. (1999). *Educating new Americans: Immigrant lives and learning*. Mahwah, NJ: Lawrence Erlbaum Associates.

Hudspeth, W. (1937). *Stone gateway and the flowery Miao*. London: Cargate.

Koltyk, J. (1998). *New pioneers in the heartland: Hmong life in Wisconsin*. Allyn & Bacon.

Livo, N., & Cha, D. (1991). *Folk stories of the Hmong: Peoples of Laos, Thailand and Vietnam*. Englewood, CO: Libraries Unlimited, Inc.

Moore, D. (1989). *Dark sky, dark land: Stories of the Hmong boy scouts of troop 100*. Eden Prarie, MN: Tessera Publishing.

Roop, P., & Roop, C. (1990). *The Hmong in America: We sought refuge here*. Appleton, WI: Appleton Area School District.

Santoli, A. (1988). *New Americans: An oral history*. New York: Viking.

Tapp, N. (1989a). Hmong religion. *Asian folklore studies, 48*, 59–94.

Tapp, N. (1989b). The impact of missionary Christianity upon marginalized ethnic minorities: The case of the Hmong. *Journal of Southeast Asian Studies, 20*(1), 70–95.

Timm, J. (1994). Hmong values and American education. *Equity and Excellence in Education, 27*(2), 36–44.

Trueba, H., Jacobs, L., & Kirton, E. (1990). *Cultural conflict and adaptation: The case of Hmong children in American society*. New York: Falmer Press.

Ungar, S. (1995). *Fresh blood: The new American immigrants*. New York: Simon & Schuster.

Vang, C., Yang, G., & Smalley, W. (1990). *The life of Shong Lue Yang: Hmong "mother of writing."* Southeast Asian refugee studies (Occasional Paper No. 9). Minneapolis: Southeast Asian Refugee Studies.

Vang, L., & Lewis, J. (1990). *Grandmother's path, grandfather's way: Oral lore, generation to generation*. Rancho Cordova, CA: Vang & Lewis.

Web Sites

Hmg magazine. http://www.hmgmagazine.com

Hmong culture and traditions. http://www.atrax.net.au/userdir/yeulee/ahtmpages/culture.htm

Hmong station. http://www.geocities.com/Tokyo/Towers/4957/index.html

Hmong tragedy. http://www.athenet.net/-jlindsay/Hmong_tragedy.html

Hmong, A unique people by topics. http://www.angelcities.com/members/hmongunivers/ topics.html

Hmong universe, a unique people. http://www.hmonguniverse.com

Lauj Youth Society. http://www.hmongyouth.org/

LaoNet's community homepage. http://www.global.lao.net/

WWW Hmong home page. http://www.hmongnet.org

4

A Mexican Family

THE CURIOUS WEDDING
OF TIJUANA (AUNT JUANA)
AND UNCLE SAM

In April, 1998, while attending an education conference in San Diego, California, I decided to make a day trip down to the Mexican border. The train going south was filled with a handful of tourists and a large number of Mexican laborers, heading home from a long night of work in *el Norte*. They were quiet, tired, and dusty, in stark contrast to the talkative, brightly colored tourists on their way to Tijuana.

Three things caught my attention at the border: The wall itself between Mexico and the United States is strong and tall, regularly patrolled by border guards on the ground and in the air. By contrast, there is a constant flow of humanity crossing the border, and mixing in the city of Tijuana. Finally, everything was for sale, from the margaritas in the plaza, to the young girls on the *Calle de la Revolucion*, to the songs played by crying children on the bridge between the two countries. The border became for me symbolic of the intimate, unforgiving, and often twisted relationship between the United States and our southern neighbors.

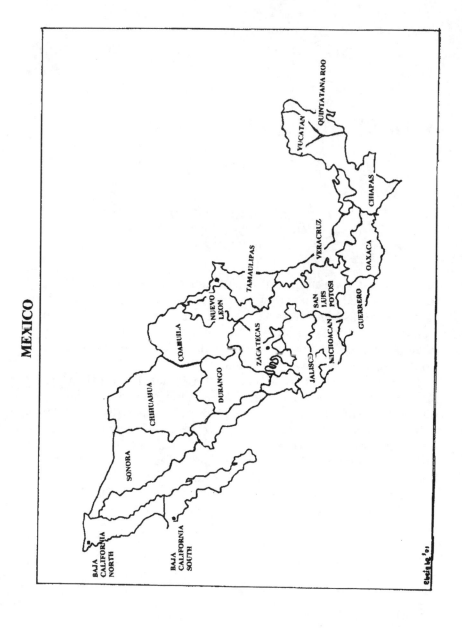

MEXICO

58

The North

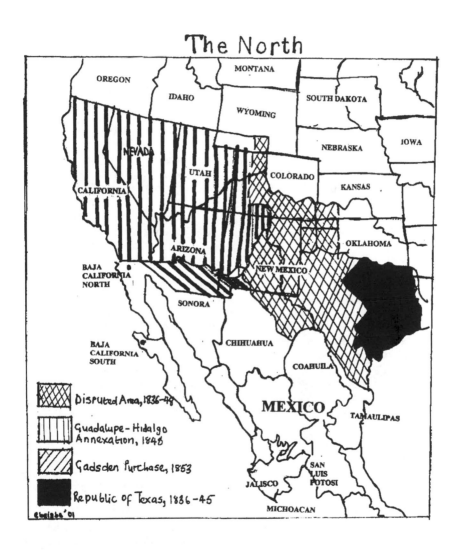

Disputed Area, 1836-48

Guadalupe-Hidalgo
Annexation, 1848

Gadsden Purchase, 1853

Republic of Texas, 1836-45

In the airport at Denver I wrote this poem, *"La Boda Curiosa de Tijuana y Tío Sam"* ["The Strange Wedding of Aunt Juana and Uncle Sam"].

De la sierra morena cielito
lindo vienen bajando
Un par de ojitos negros
cielito lindo de contrabando

De la sierra morena cielito
lindo vienen bajando
Un par de ojitos negros
cielito lindo de contrabando

Gritando, llorando,
el niño callejero
con su maltocada guitarrita
canta esa famosa canción
para entretener
los turistas ambulantes
El está sentado
al medio del puente
que se unía en matrimonio no sagrado
Tijuana y Tío Sam.

Screaming, crying,
The street child
With his little badly tuned guitar
Sings this famous song
To entertain
The wandering tourists
He is sitting
In the middle of the bridge
That unites in unHoly Matrimony
Tijuana and Uncle Sam.

El cantante es pequeñito,
color de la tierra morena,
ojitos negros,
con la física y la ropa de los
pueblos primeros,
los indios desterrados
Sus hermanos y hermanas están cercas,
algunas madres también,
sus huahuas al pecho o espalda,
quizás su pueblo entero trasladado aquí
todos pidiendo dinero
todos pequeñitos
todos hambrientos
pero jugando sus papeles
en esta ceremonia no sagrada
a la zona del libre comercio
entre Tijuana y Tío Sam.

The singer is small,
The color of the brown earth,
Black eyes,
With the physique and clothing
Of the First Peoples,
The Indians without Lands
His brothers and sisters are nearby
Some mothers, too,
Their babies at their chest or their back,
Perhaps their entire village has moved here
Everyone is asking for money
They are all so small
They are all so hungry
But they continue to play their parts
In this unholy ceremony
In the free trade zone between
Tijuana and Uncle Sam.

Todos aquí son buenos actores
desde los cantineros en los cafés
"Are you ready for your margarita yet,
amigo?"
y los vendedores de artesanías o carne
humano
por la Avenida de la Revolución
"Come on in, *amigo*—
Take a look at the naked girls."

Everybody here is a good actor
From the barkers in the cafes
"Are you ready for your margarita yet,
amigo?"
and the sellers of crafts and
human flesh
on Revolucion Avenue
"Come on in, *amigo*—
Take a look at the naked girls."

Avenida de la Revolución—
¿Por esa tramposa mentira lucharon
Emiliano Zapata y Pancho Villa?
Hasta los niños
quienes venden su niñez
y la patromonia cultural de su país
a los turistas—
This is Free Trade, *hombre*
y aquí todos pueden aprovechar
todos son libres de vender sus tierras,
sus casas, sus trabajos,
sus culturas, sus cuerpos,
sus niños, sus vidas
a los compradores

El turista, también, tiene su papel—
consiste en ambular, mirar, comprar
cuidar sus dólares
"Are these real Cuban cigars, *hombre?*
How can I get them past the border guard?"
y tomar fotos
Algunos se acercan al niño indio
"Can you get a shot of me with him,
Gladis?
Isn't he cute?"
No se les occuren que el niño llorando
su canción de alegría
puede ser su hijo, su hermano

Al fondo de la foto
el puente que se unía
las casas amontanadas de Mexico
las torres brillantes de los Estados
Unidos,
hechos por las mismas manos morenas,
y, más allá, el sol y
un cielito aún lindo
hasta la naturaleza se ríe
y participa en esta curiosa y maldita boda
de Tijuana y Tío Sam

Mira ... se acercan los músicos:
Ay, ay, ay, ay
cantan, no llores,
porque cantando se alegran
Cielito Lindo los corazones

Revolution Avenue—
Is this the lie for which
Emiliano Zapata and Pancho Villa fought?
Even the children
Sell their childhood
And the cultural heritage of their country
To the tourists—
This Is Free Trade, man
And here everyone can profit
Everyone is free to sell their lands,
Their houses, their labor,
Their cultures, their bodies,
Their children, their lives,
To the highest bidder

The tourist also has his role
It consists of wandering about, looking,
buying, watching his money,
"Are these real Cuban cigars, man?
How can I get them past the border guard?"
And taking photos
Some tourists close in on a little Indian boy
"Can you get a shot of me with him,
Gladis?
Isn't he cute?"
It doesn't occur to them that the child
crying out his happy song
could be their son, their brother

In the background of the photo
Is the bridge that unites
The crowded, jumbled-up houses of Mexico
And the brilliant towers of the United
States
Both made by the same brown hands
And, further off, the sun, and
A sky still pretty
Even nature laughs and participates in this
curious and damnable wedding of
Aunt Juana and Uncle Sam.

Look ... here come the musicians:
Ay, ay, ay, ay
cantun, no llores,
porque cantando se alegran
Cielito Lindo los corazones

LA FRONTERA

Mexico's people have endured a conquest at the hands of the Europeans and their descendants that goes back to 1519 and the arrival of Hernan Cortez. Three hundred years of Spanish rule were followed by a brief period of independence for Mexico, until the United States renewed the conquest. The Texas war in 1835 and the war in Mexico from 1846 to 1848 were driven by a philosophy of manifest destiny, wherein the United States assumed a God-given right to the lands of its neighbors. These two wars resulted in Mexico's loss of over half of its national territory, and helped to send the United States on its way to becoming a world political and economic power.

Other nations were not far behind in despoiling Mexico of its resources. During the dictatorship of Porfirio Diaz in the late 1800s, England, France, and the United States gained substantial holdings in Mexican mining operations, banks, railroads, oil, and agricultural, and forest lands. This wholesale takeover of Mexico was checked by the revolution of 1911–1919, but in the revolution's aftermath, and in the long rule of the Institutional Revolutionary Party (IRP), the United States has taken the lead in this annexation of "Mexico's political, social, cultural, and, most of all, economic turf" (Ross, 1998).

With much of their country in the hands of foreign investors, and with their own political leadership removed from the daily struggle for survival they face, many millions of Mexicans have made the journey to the north, to work in the *maquilladora* plants on the border, or further yet, to seek economic opportunity in the United States. Workers on the border make parts for U.S. corporations, which would have to pay many times more for the same labor in the United States. Mexican workers are enticed to the United States to pick crops, work in packing plants, and perform other labor for wages well below that paid to other Americans. Often they find themselves working for the same corporate entities in the United States that they had worked for before in Mexico, but for better wages. Mexicans, with or without documents, continue to receive a poor welcome from border guards, police, and average citizens. Those with dark skins and heavy accents make special targets in a land where skin color and language continue to mark people for ill treatment.

Newly arrived Mexican immigrants are here for work, and workers worldwide face grim realities in these days of global markets. Chomsky (1994) wrote:

> [The] internationalization of production provides multinational corporations with new weapons to undermine working people in the West. Workers must now accept an end to their "luxurious" lifestyles and agree to "flexibility

of labor markets" (i.e., not knowing whether you have a job tomorrow) ... The attack on worker rights, social standards, and functioning democracy throughout the world reflects this new economic order. (pp. 175–176)

It was not coincidence that the passage of the North Atlantic Free Trade Agreement (NAFTA) in Mexico and the United States in January, 1994, was accompanied by the beginning of the Zapatista Rebellion in Southeast Mexico. Serving as a forum for democratic expression, the Zapatistas brought to the world's attention the human dimension of transnational capitalism. Ancestral lands held by indigenous people could be bought up by international developers; millions of Mexicans were expected to lose their jobs in the first 5 years of the accord. A short time after the NAFTA vote in the U.S. Congress, "workers were fired from Mexican Honeywell and GE plants for attempting to organize independent unions" (Chomsky, 1994, p. 179). Clearly, the large-scale immigration of Mexicans to northeastern Wisconsin and elsewhere in the United States is fueled by the ransacking of their native land by forces of transnational capital. At the same time, these newly arrived workers encounter the distrust and open animosity of U.S. workers who have seen their jobs and factories "go South," all in the name of "flexibility of labor markets."

As more and more Mexican immigrants arrive in Fox Valley, Wisconsin in search of economic opportunity, teachers are challenged to find ways to communicate effectively with children and their parents. To date, few bilingual programs exist in area districts, and few teachers, administrators or counselors are fluent in Spanish. Accepting this challenge, Maya Song-Goede, an ESL teacher, and Judy Mehn, a graduate student, interview the mother of one of Ms. Song-Goede's students. Angela Gonzales and some members of her family have recently relocated to Oshkosh from California.

FIG. 4.1.   Judy Mehn making tortillas with Angela Gonzales,
April 1999, Oshkosh, Wisconsin.

FIG. 4.2.   Maya Song-Goede and Angela Gonzales preparing food.

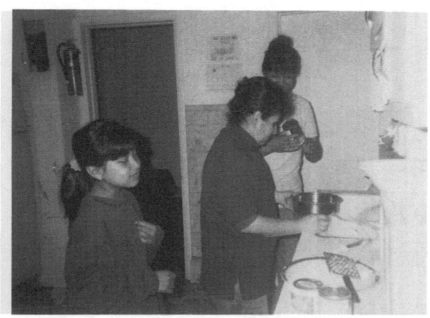

FIG. 4.3.   Angela Gonzales, her daughter, and Rosa Gonzales Ramirez, in Angela's kitchen, April 1999.

— THE GONZALES FAMILY —

*Judy Mehn and Maya Song-Goede
With Angela Gonzales*

The history of Angela took us to a place and time of hard labor, submissive wives, and little money. A place where children make their own toys so they would have something to play with, and a time consumed with daily chores, leaving no time for storytelling with the children. No time for leisure outside of family reunions. The place for socialization was limited to recess time at school, that is, if the children were privileged enough to attend. Yet, the hard work that built Angela's childhood left no streak of remorse. Pride was her foundation and the values of her family strengthened her resiliency.

Angela Gonzales is a petite woman in her early 40s. She was born in Culiacan, Sinaloa, Mexico. She came to the United States in 1976 and lived in North Ridge, California. Her second husband, Jesus Gonzales, was born in Uroapan, Michoacan, Mexico. Jesus is 3 years her junior. She met both of her husbands in California. Her first husband died, leaving her with their two sons, Ricardo and Hector. Many years later, Angela met and married Jesus. They are considered married to their families and the Mexican community, but are not legally married as defined by the law. Together they had her youngest son, Sergio. Her sons are 19, 18, and 7.

In July of 1955, Jesus came to Oshkosh, Wisconsin, to work in a Mexican restaurant. The employer who recruited him promised a job and a place for his family to live until they could make enough to support themselves. A month later, the rest of the family joined him. Angela was also given a job as a waitress at the Mexican restaurant. As soon as they saved enough money, they moved into an apartment of their own. Unfortunately for Jesus, the Mexican restaurant was not successful and closed down. Even though Jesus' job venture turned sour, they have a lot to be thankful for. Jesus is currently working in another Mexican restaurant and Angela is back at work in a factory.

As we sit around her dining room table, Angela shared with us her journey to America, encounter with discrimination, responsibility as a parent, and hopes for the family and future. Angela's sister-in-law, Rosa, has also been present at every interviewing visit.

Rosa Gonzales Ramirez is a tall, dark, pretty Mexican woman. She does not speak much English, so Angela and Rosa's oldest daughter, Martha, did all the translation for us. Rosa is married and has three children: Martha,

Carlos, and Lorena. Martha is 17 and is currently in high school; Carlos is 11 and Lorena is 9, and they are both in elementary school.

Rosa and her husband came to Los Angeles, California, with his uncle in January, 1992. They came here looking for better jobs that could offer them a better life, even though they knew very little English. The children were left behind with grandparents while Rosa and her husband worked diligently to earn enough money to bring them across the border. In the fall of 1993, they finally saved enough money to bring the children over. In order to bring the children across the border, they had to pay someone to provide visas for them. That person would look for another family with the same number of children and use their visas. Then they would pack the car and have the children sitting in the back seats. They would drive around until the children fell asleep before they would cross the border. When they go through customs, the officials ask for the visas and check to make sure there are no trespassers. The children would pass by easily since they were sleeping. This was how the children came here. In September 1998, Rosa and her husband decided to move to Wisconsin to join Angela's family. Despite the cold winter, her family is slowly adjusting to the homogeneous city of Oshkosh.

Culiacan, Mexico

Angela remembers her homeland as a place filled with beauty. It was clean and nice. The only problem was the fact that her family had no money. She lived with her father, mother, and two half sisters. Her father worked in the field and her mother stayed at home. They lived in one big room, which included a kitchen, living room, and a dining room. There was no bathroom. Eventually, by the time she turned 14, her father acquired government land from his job to build a two bedroom brick house with a shower. Her father took several years to build the house, one room at a time. According to Angela, this was considered "high class" because owning a home was rare.

In Mexico, the people who still work on farms grow tomatoes, chiles, mangos, and various vegetables. Angela commented that most of the produce was transported to the United States and the leftovers were given to the Mexican people. Her face quickly brightened up with pride as she stated that the farms were owned by the Mexican people.

The Agrarian Reform Act of 1915 and the constitution of 1917 laid the foundation for changes in Mexico's tenure system (Merrill & Miro, 1997). These documents established that the nation retained ultimate control over privately held land and the right to redistribute it (Merrill & Miro, 1997). *Ejidos*, are communally farmed plots developed as the government redistributed large land holdings (Merrill & Miro, 1997). Under this arrangement, the people could petition the government to seize private properties and expropriate them. The state retained the title, but the people were allowed to farm the land (Merrill & Miro, 1997). Though the intention of the *ejido* was good, it eventually created problems because 31% of the farmers did not farm enough land to support a family (Merrill & Miro, 1997).

Angela described her parents as very strict. She said they wanted the children to be submissive and obedient. They could not question or talk back to their parents.

The roles of girls and boys are clearly defined in Mexican families. Even though she did not have a brother, she was able to take on the different roles that were expected from each. The boys in the family had the responsibility of looking out for their family. It was not unusual to see 5- and 6-year-old boys selling gum on the street. If they were old enough, they had to work in the field. The girls' role was to help their mother's with household chores. Angela even explained that her older sisters were not allowed to have boyfriends because it was considered a big sin. There were a lot of girls who did not marry because of this. This same rule did not apply to the boys. It was acceptable for them to date as many girls as they wanted.

Life was difficult and there was little time to play. Most of Angela's time was spent going to school and helping around the house. There was always so much to do because most chores were done by hand. They also had to make their own clothes because money was tight. She had to learn how to knit and sew. Angela's family never owned a television, so when they wanted to watch TV, they had to pay the neighbor 20¢.

Despite duties around the house, Angela did manage to attend and finish a secondary school program, which is equivalent to the high school program in the United States. It was during this time that she learned English. In Mexico, there are public schools available for the people. They begin with primary school (Grades 1–6), a 3-year secondary or vocational education program, and a mid-level education through a 3-year college preparatory program or advance technical training. Four year colleges and post-graduate training are also available for those who are fortunate enough to attend (Merrill & Miro, 1997). I was surprised that she was able to finish high school because education did not seem to be a necessity with many poor Mexican families. According to a 1989 government report, 880,000 students dropped out of primary school and 30% of all secondary school enrollers failed to complete the 3-year curriculum (Merrill & Miro, 1997).

Angela's family did not have a lot of celebrations. On Sundays, they would visit her grandparents and have a dinner consisting of beans, tortillas, and chiles. On occasions, they would have beef soup. They celebrated *Las Posadas*, *La Navidad*, Ash Wednesday, Mother's Day, New Year's Day, and Lent. *Las Posadas* is a celebration of the birth of Christ. It lasts for several days and the people reenact the holy birth. *La Navidad* is celebrated on December 24th and includes a big supper. We asked Angela about *Cinco de Mayo*, the Anniversary of the Battle of Puebla, but she said it was not celebrated in Mexico. She considers it a commercial holiday.

When asked if she was happy in Mexico, she said, "When you don't know nothing about life, you are happy with what you have."

Time Line

This is not a complete timeline of Angela's life. The purpose of this is to aid in the understanding of events that happened after she came to the United States.

1976	Angela comes to the United States to visit her sister in California for 1 month and goes back home. In another month, she comes back to stay with her sister and does not return to Mexico for 10 years.
Early 1977	Angela gets her social security card and finds a job sewing and knitting in a factory.
1978	Angela works at Lago Landrina (The Swallow Restaurant).
April, 1979	Ricardo is born.
April, 1980	Hector is born.
1986	Congress passes a new immigration bill allowing amnesty to all aliens who entered the United States before January 1, 1982 (Ashabranner, 1987)
1989	Angela works at La Parrilla (The Grill) and meets Jesus.
1990	Angela and Jesus move in together.
August, 1991	Sergio is born.
July, 1995	Jesus comes to Oshkosh, Wisconsin.
August, 1995	Angela and the rest of the family come to Oshkosh. The live in a place provided by their employer. Both Jesus and Angela work at a Mexican restaurant.
September, 1995	The family moves into an apartment.
December, 1995	Angela goes to work in a factory in Appleton through a temporary employment agency.
July, 1996	The family moves to a house because of a bad experience with a landlord.
1997	Angela begins working at a factory in Neenah, Wisconsin.

Transition to America

A lot is inevitably going to change in a life when removing it from the place of its origin. Urrea (1993) beautifully and graphically uses words to paint the dirty canvas of the border as he opens our eyes to the meaning behind the move itself:

> It seems jolly on the page. But imagine poverty, violence, natural disasters, or political fear driving you away from everything you know. Imagine how bad things get to make you leave behind your family, your friends, your lovers; your home, as humble as it might be; your church, say. Let's take it further—you've said good-bye to the graveyard, the dog, the goat, the mountains where you first hunted, your grade school, your state, your favorite spot on the river where you fished and took time to think.
>
> Then you come hundreds—or thousands—of miles across territory utterly unknown to you. (Chances are, you have never traveled farther than a hundred miles in your life.) You have walked, run, hidden in the backs of trucks, spent part of your precious money on bus fare. There is no AAA or Travelers Aid Society available to you. Various features of your journey north might include police corruption; violence in the forms of beatings, rape, murder, torture, road accidents; theft; incarceration. Additionally, you might experience loneliness, fear, exhaustion, sorrow, cold, heat, diarrhea, thirst, hunger. There is no medical attention available to you. There isn't even Kotex. (p. 38)

These words by Urrea provide insight into the immigrants' excitement over reaching America, on the acceptance of low status positions in American society, on their perseverance in the face of discrimination.

Angela speaks of her transition to America:

> My sister wrote a letter
> Said I wanted to come
> I didn't even think about it
> It was like a vacation
> My parents didn't realize …
> It was November
> I can remember the day
> My sister wanted to pick me up
> in Tijuana
> It was so nice
> My first experience
> American people

touristic
Mexican food
I spent the day there
By afternoon we cross the border
Big difference
A lot of highways
Buildings so different
It was those days where
With the police
You feel protected
So nice
So clean
So different
In Mexico people don't respect you
They say bad things to you
Or grab you
I stayed for over a month, and then
Back to Mexico
I decided to come for vacation ... again
I didn't go back until
Ten years later
I told my parents it was a vacation
Otherwise
They would not let me come back again.

Dialogue

Judy: How long did the trip take?

Angela: It was 24 hours from my state to the border and then it was about 2½ hours from the border to LA.

Judy: You said your sister came down to pick you up?

Angela: She drove down the whole way.

Judy: But they don't give her problems about crossing the border?

Angela: No. She was resident at that time. Legal resident. Because she was crossing [when] people [were] just a little confused. Like, if they don't know the status, [then] we are legal residents, we are not citizens. Then after a certain time, after we got the green card, 5 years later you can apply for citizenship.

Maya: I know what that is. My parents came in 1979 or 1980 and we were legal residents too, but we came as refugees. So we had green cards and everything ...

Angela: So as soon as you got here you are resident ...?

Maya: My parents ... we have citizenship now.

Angela: Because after I got my passport for a month, then after a month I become illegal. I just stay illegal for [a long time].

Judy: Because the visa or the passport expires?

Angela: The visa expires. Exactly.

Maya: At that time they didn't give you any problems about it.

Angela: No. When I came I decided to look for a job. Course those days it was easy to get a social security card so you just have to write by mail and they just send it to you, so there was no problem to look for a job, and in those days you look for a job, and you find it.

Maya: Did you have to get a green card too?

Angela: No. If you are looking for a job, they just ask for your social security card. They don't ask if you are a resident or not, legal or illegal, they don't care. They just want someone to work for them.

Maya: They aren't as strict as they are now.

Angela: Well, in those years you had to be very careful on the street. [They would stop you while you were resting at the bus stops], or they used to go to the factories, and you just had to run. But, you know everybody was so nice and they just let us know. I think they let them know when the immigration is going to the factory. The owner would tell us.

The first time that I came here, I could not walk on the street ... I can, but I was afraid to get stopped anytime. Or on the bus stop, we can stay on the bus stop just waiting for the bus, you just have to be hiding and see the bus, and take it. There was a lot of immigration, a lot of immigration in those days. I remember I used to carry like a magazine or the newspaper and I was reading like an American newspaper (she holds up a newspaper and pretends to be reading, covering her face behind American print) Ha, ha! Yeah, because it was awful. Those years were awful!

Judy: So after your visa expired the next step you took toward residency ... or to become a legal resident was ...

Angela: No, not at all. Even then, when I was married the first time, I did not think to become a resident. Because I even had the kids and I didn't start looking for the records. Because Mexican people are always thinking that they are going back. "No, I don't want to be resident because I am going back next year." That is the song for every day. Next year I am going to be back. We never do.

Maya: Rosa, what did you feel when you came to Wisconsin? What were some big changes?

Angela: (translating for Rosa): She said she makes more money here than in California, so the jobs are better, and the rent [is] more money [in California]. Like when you pay $900 in California, you pay $500 here. So it is why we like it better over here.

According to Angela, the transition to Wisconsin was very different and much more difficult for her than it was for Rosa because when Rosa moved to Wisconsin, Angela was there to help her out. When Angela came, there was no family, no support, nothing.

Maya: Did you move [to Wisconsin] because Jesus's family was over here?

Rosa: Yes.

Maya: Do you have any other family that lives here?

Angela: No.

Maya: Rosa, how do you think about the people ... I know that [Angela] said a lot of people were prejudiced because they're not used to seeing a lot of Mexicans.

Angela: The thing is she came with us. We introduced her to other Mexican families. It was hard for me. I was telling Martha (Rosa's oldest daughter) that when I came here, for the cold, no one give us gloves or hats or warmers, nothing. We did it with [Rosa's family] because we know that they don't have nothing like that. When we came, we didn't know what to buy or where to get it for less money, or something like that, where to shop or where to go. We didn't know where the stores were, and there were no other Mexicans around here.

In time, familiarity became a friend to the Gonzales family. Angela eventually connected with a few other Mexican families in Oshkosh. The children met friends at school and became involved in activities provided in their community. So their lives changed and the influences of the American culture are strong as the Gonzales family connected with a new way of life found in the small city of Oshkosh. Employment positions and standards of living are better. Material things were available for Angela's children that she herself couldn't have hoped for in her own childhood.

Discrimination

Angela made it clear that the hardest transition was not migrating to California, it was moving from California to Wisconsin. Some of the reasoning behind this was because of the unexpected weather. No one had informed them of the long winters and they had not come dressed for the occasion. However, discrimination chilled them more than Wisconsin's most bitter winter. We have gathered from our interview dialogue a few cases of discrimination and offer some examples of racial tension experienced first hand by Angela:

At Work:

Angela: Here in Wisconsin I feel that there was a lot of discrimination at the time that I come. [When] most people noticed that I didn't speak good English, they started making fun of us, or asking, "Where you from," or "Do you have papers?" "Are you legal or not?"

Maya: You mean employers would ask you?

Angela: Employers and sometimes customers. [Imitating White American customers] "How you come to Wisconsin?" or "What are you doing in Wisconsin? It's only White people." ... Well, I'm legal, so I can be anywhere in the United States.

She experienced great tension working as a waitress in Wisconsin. It didn't take long before she made the decision to leave waitressing behind her forever. She said she would never waitress in Wisconsin again. It is interesting to point out that in California, she waitressed for over 16 years with no problems. Ironically, Angela encouraged her husband to pursue the new position at the Mexican restaurant in Wisconsin. Angela confided, however, that her husband's job wasn't as stressful in terms of discrimination because he was a cook and cooks didn't have to deal with the customers so much. It is also fascinating to find that all of the discriminatory dialogue taken from our interview is set in Wisconsin, with not one example of discrimination shared with us from her 18 years spent in California.

Angela: When I started working at [the Mexican restaurant] as a waitress, I used to go to the tables and as soon as the people see me, instead of saying "Hi" or "Hello" they said, "Oh, no Spanish!" I said, "Well, I'm not going to speak in Spanish, I'm going to try to speak in English." And they say, "Oh, you speak English?" and I said, "Well, I'll try!"
[Working in the factory], if you don't speak English right, forget it. You're lost. But one thing that I noticed ... If I work by myself I am okay. Even the White people [are] close, and they talk to me, and they want to make me feel like I am at home. But I notice that when there are two or more Mexicans, they try to keep away. Like, for example, if we are speaking in Spanish ... the White people goes, "What are you saying?" And I say something like, "I don't know. We were just talking." And they say, "Did you say something about me?" I don't know. They always think that we are talking about them.... But I noticed that anyplace that I have been by myself, if I am the only Spanish speaking, they go to me and they talk, and they want to make me feel better.

At Home:

Angela: When we first came, the owner of the restaurant gave us a place to live. After 2 months they said you have to go and look for your own apartment, and he gave us some money for renting.

Judy: Was it like a loan, or did he offer it to you?

Angela: He offered it to us. We had a nice apartment, but we were kicked out. They kicked us out. One day my son was fixing the car, the tire of the car, and he left it on the jack, he went into the house. The manager came and said, "I don't want you to leave the car like that." And so, okay, so we put the tire back and that's it.... After that, the manager, she used to go by the apartment, and she was just watching us like that [tight lipped, suspicious expression] and my kids, back then one was 14 and the other one was 15 and he used to say, "Hey, why are you looking at me like that?" and he goes, "Excuse me," "Oh, shut up." He says. So it was in the morning, the morning after, I got a paper saying that I have to move out, that I have 3 days to move out. So we feel very discriminated against by the manager. My son didn't like it that she was looking around or telling things to us. I don't know for what reason he went to the apartment at eight o'clock in the morning and I usually work third shift so I was asleep and he just surprised me, knocking very strong.... It was a Christmas tree or something that somebody [threw in the street] and he thought it was ours because we can't have the real ones. And he went to say to me ... but he just talk. I was just shocked because he goes, "Oh, I don't want you to have a Christmas tree, and you know, blah, blah, blah, and the fire regulations." And I said, "Oh. Okay." So when my kids came home I told them what happened, and one of the kids saw him in the apartment and said, "You know what? I don't want you to go and wake up my mom at eight o'clock. Whenever you have something to tell her you should go later because she works third shift." And he didn't like it. He gave us a notice to leave the apartment. Three days notice. And I started looking for another apartment, and I was on a waiting list, or something like that, for 3 months, so there was no way to find someplace else to live. I went to the manager and I told her there is no way to move out, and just like that we have a contract for 1 year so they can not just kick us out for nothing. She gave me a letter saying that I have to move out and the police was notified of what happened. And I said what happened? I didn't even know what was the reason, so I went and talked to her and I said, "You know what? You don't even know how you put people out on the street." Because if she gives me a month I can go find a place, but in 3 days! There was no way to go and nowhere to go. And I said, "You know what? I have my contract so you cannot kick me out."

Judy: Did the police try to back you up?

Angela: No. Nobody. I just went to talk to her. And the police didn't even know what happened. It was just that she was trying to scare us.

Judy: So you didn't have to move out.

Angela: No, because everything she gave me was in writing. So I had that letter, and the contract, it was 2 months left. So a month later I got another letter saying that there was no new contract for us. So we have to leave at that time. So after that we were not happy there, so we start looking for a house. We find this one, and we move, I guess, on the 12th of July so we had plenty of time to clean the apartment (the contract expired in September). We did everything. We *clean* it. Clean, clean, clean. So we can go clean. So I called her so she could come see the apartment and see what I left because I don't want any problems after that. We left only one spot on the carpet and she said, "Well, there is a spot right here and I think I want to change it ..." And I said okay. So after that I got a letter, while I was here in this house, I got a letter that I owe her $1,600 because she changed the carpet. And I said, "Oh, my God!" She didn't give us a deposit back. But I don't want to sue her because it was going to be for money. And I say, money? What for?

Maya: Did you have to pay her?

Angela: No, she was saying that trying to scare us. But she got very scared when I told her, "If you want to kick me out I want to go to court." She was so racist. And I find out, now, she doesn't take any more Mexicans.

Language and Culture:

Maya: You said in California you didn't have to speak English because a lot of people spoke Spanish. Were the White people, were they speaking Spanish, too?

Angela: Most of the people, yeah.

Maya: Were they a lot friendlier than the people here?

Angela: Yes. And they know how to talk to us. For example, if they speak English, they try to speak it slow, or with their [gestures], they help us a lot. But not here. People here, they just talk. If you understand, fine. If you don't, you lose it.

In Sam's Club in Appleton, there was a Hmong couple, and there was a White couple, and the White people were looking at the Hmong, and I was looking at the Whites! You know, Hmong people, like Mexicans, most of them, they are shorter. And [the Whites] were looking at them like some like the strangest things! I never seen Hmong people before, because Hmong are different than the Chinese in California, or the Japanese. Hmong are so different. But who cares? They have two eyes, one mouth, one head. They think.

Judy: I grew up in Madison, Wisconsin, and I know there is a lot of diversity in the state capital of Wisconsin. I lived around it, I saw it, and to my knowledge I was never prejudiced, but my parents and extended family were. It made me very angry growing up. There was a lot of tension there ... but I was wondering why, why is there this difference? Why am I so open and much of my family isn't? My parents had no intention of teaching me to be prejudiced. They wanted me to be open to other cultures, yet, they didn't practice that. I thought about this for years. What I have come to believe is that so many people, at least in my family, just don't want to get to know another culture. Anything different from them they're afraid of (although they would never admit they are afraid). They are afraid of what they do not know, and of what they do not come to know.

Angela: You know, even some Mexicans that I met here, they don't speak Spanish at all. And I ask why? In California, for example, White people hire Spanish speaking people to work in the houses so the kids can learn Spanish. So they grow with English and Spanish. And here [in Wisconsin] people say, "Spanish? What for?"

Despite the ill-intended feelings many people impressed on Angela as she made a life for herself and for her family in Wisconsin, she has no regrets about living in Wisconsin, and doesn't wish to return to California. With family so far away in California, and after hearing shocking stories about the community that surrounds me, I was surprised to hear that she felt her relocation to Wisconsin was a great move. She definitely makes more money here than she would in California, and can buy more for the dollar with the money she makes because the cost of living is so high in California. She also feels safer in Wisconsin, where there is less crime and drugs.

Angela at one point stated, "We come to America and we go to work doing all these jobs that we do not like when we are in Mexico (cleaning bathrooms, etc.). Maybe it's okay in America because you get more money for the jobs." Rosa, on the other hand, says she was waiting for her life to get better, and she hasn't seen it yet. She mentions, "the good life" in America, and we all laugh.

Encounters With Culture and Language

Maya and I listened to Angela as she described her first experiences working in America. America was an extremely exciting place for her to be, and she opened her eyes to many new experiences. Angela was not only exposed to new lifestyles, but to a new knowledge of other cultures as well. Angela recalls one particular experience as she works at her first job at a factory in America:

> You know, I never knew Cuban people. I never mingle with American people. Even Mexicans. We are Mexicans but we come from different states. So it was like a new world for me. But I met a Cuban lady, she was White with blue eyes! And I never thought it was like that. White people in Cuba! Because in Mexico there are a lot of Cubans but they are Black. I got so excited, I said are you Cuban? I didn't know there was White people in Cuba. Because I told her in Mexico it's only Black. And she said, "Yeah, the Black ones go to Mexico and the White people come to the United States." I thought Oh, okay. You know, people that are in Culiacan and people that are in Michoacan, they are so different. People from the south, they can do a lot of things by hand, they can do sewing by hand, they can do pots, they can do everything. Not on the other side. And then, even if we were Mexicans, we were different. A lot of difference. And the job it was … I don't know, it was something that I liked to do, just working and talking, how long have you been here, are you married, are you single … but I like it.

We asked Angela to elaborate on how people from Culiacan are so different from people from Michoacan. She compared the cultures of the north (Culiacan) to the cultures of the south (Michoacan). The north she described as "more fancy," with machines and more technology. She thought the north to be a place where people lived a better life. In the south, the people were behind the times, keeping old customs. A *molcajete* (stone bowl) is used to blend food. Stone is also used at the place where clothes are washed by hand. Although Angela is true to the character she brought with her to America, she admits, "When we are in America, we don't act like Mexicans. It is a different kind of life. We change a little bit."

Angela speaks of her school days and learning English:

> Mexican people
> we come to work
> We have no time to go to school
> I used to go and register
> One week or two weeks and then
> Oh God!
> I'm so tired!
> I'm not gonna do it
> When I learned
> I went to LA
> It was a good, good school
> They want you to speak

> Smart teacher, that lady
> She teaches a conversation every day
> Conversation, conversation
> In the laundry
> In the market
> In the airport
> In the house ...
> Things that you are going to need
> She was English only
> But she let us know
> Using her hands
> And things like that
> For that time
> Schools wanted you to speak English
> Now
> My husband, his brother
> He goes to school
> Education in Mexico
> Two or three years
> They're teaching him grammar
> He doesn't know in Spanish
> How can he know in English?
> We get so confused
> The thing is
> We want to *speak*
> I was lucky to go to that school.

Angela recommends that teachers of the English language teach how we talk to others. The need for relevance is extremely necessary when immigrants are learning a foreign language.

Parenting

Moving to another country in search of a better life has proven, for Angela, to be a favorable challenge as long as she could raise her children and provide for them. We discussed with Angela her views on parenting and how it has changed. During this process, we had assumed responses that would include methods and reasons. What we discovered was that her vision of parenting can be described more as a lifestyle. This seems to parallel with Valdes's explanation of *consejos*, which are "spontaneous homilies designed to influence behaviors and attitudes" (Valdes, 1996). Angela feels that parenting here has changed little because she has not adopted the American style of raising children. Like any caring parent, she does her best to raise her three sons.

Maya: What do you do that's different from American families?
Angela: [The children] have to let us know where they are going, when
they're going to be back, who are they with. We try to know
what they are doing, if they are throwing a party, is there gonna
be beer or not ... We try to know.
Judy: Do you have a curfew? At what time do they have to be home?
Angela: Before twelve, but when I started to work third shift, I started to
lose control of my older sons. Because I left to work and I didn't
know if they were home or not. One day on a weekend I went
home and nobody was there. The three of them were gone, my
nephew and two sons. They came later. "And where were you?"
"Oh, I just went to buy cigarettes." "At four in the morning?"
Judy: So you think some of your parenting abilities were lost because
you had to work certain hours or the many hours?
Angela: Only at night. Because [when] I left home they were home, but I
don't know if they stay at home or not.

Angela has tried to use parenting techniques similar to what her parents
used. She believes children should live at home and abide by the guidelines
she has set. They do not gain their independence until they are married.
Even after they are married, if they are living under her roof, they should follow her rules. Her older sons have been anxious to be independent from her
and tried moving out. She has discouraged this because they continue to
move back home. She used her oldest son as an example. Ricardo has
moved out several times already. He just moved out again and is now thinking about moving back in. It is evident that she wants the best she can afford
for her children. In return she asks for respect and appreciation. As she now
explains, this is something that has been difficult for her children to show her.

Judy: I was wondering if you felt that *respeto* in Mexico is different
from respect here. Some White American parents here want to
have their children respect them, but do you feel that this kind of
respect is different?
Angela: In Mexico, the kids know that when they grow and work they
have to help their parents. Here in the United States, they don't
have to help their parents. So the American style is they can
move out because they have everything, they have nothing to
give back to their parents. In Mexico, we feel like we have to pay
back because our parents give us a lot.
Judy: Do you think that will continue in your family?
Angela: No, because they grow in American style. See, I try to be like
Mexico, but I can't. Too much TV, influences, and their friends.
Judy: So some values that you've brought to America have changed
since you've moved here?

Angela: Yeah … with the kids, they don't appreciate. I feel like they don't appreciate what I did for them. When they were little, the two older ones, I use to have two jobs and I never went out, I never do nothing because I have to work. They had no father so I have to take care of the house, to pay the rent, to buy the clothes for them, and it seems like they don't care. It seems like they don't … feel like I work for them. They think it was my responsibility to have everything for them.

Despite her children's perceived lack of appreciation for what she has done for them, Angela still works hard to give them the material things that she was never privileged to have as a child. This was very important to her. She remembers the feeling of not having a doll in Mexico. It was a feeling that she does not want her children to experience.

Besides respect and appreciation, discipline is also an important part of raising children. For Angela, discipline included corporal punishment. Spanking was a way to discipline and teach children respect. She does not spank much now, but this is not because she finds spanking objectionable. It is now the case that she fears the consequences of her actions because her children threaten to turn her in for child abuse. She expressed that now she doesn't know how to discipline. She also feels this is causing her to lose control of her children. There was a lapse of silence following this statement as her shoulders fell forward in defeat. Later, we discovered she resorted to time-outs when Sergio was very young, and a base for grounding is not unfamiliar to him in this present time. But again, Angela made it evident that much respect from her children had been lost, and the restrictions America placed on her role as a disciplinarian was a big part of this happening.

Despite dramatic changes in Mexican society since 1940, the family remains the most important social institution (Merrill & Miro, 1997). As Angela's two older sons are getting older and might one day get married and start a family, we inquired about the family values she would like them to carry on.

Maya: What are some practices that you want your children to still practice when they have their own family?

Angela: Sometimes, I feel like a they have to teach Spanish because when they have a kid and we want to go visit our family, if they don't speak Spanish they won't be able to speak to the relatives in Mexico. But the thing is if they marry an American person they lose the Spanish. The Spanish language.

Maya: So, are you encouraging them not to marry a White American?

Angela: No, just to teach them Spanish or a little of the background. You know. Not to lose the Mexican heritage.

Judy: What kind of background do you want your grandchildren to have?

Angela: First, I want them to speak Spanish … it depends on the couple. Ricardo's girlfriend, she's trying to speak Spanish, she likes to cook. I teach her how to cook and she wants to learn our Mexican style. But Hector used to have a girlfriend, she doesn't like to learn how to cook, she doesn't like nothing Mexican. If she doesn't like the Mexican style, it's going to be hard for the family.

Judy: But what about values that you want them to carry with them?

Angela: Well, at least to respect their family. What I want is for them to be married like a Mexican. We don't like to have other people know about our life. Like my marriage, I don't want to have other people know what kind of problems that I have … I try to teach them that their problems are going to be their problems, their family for good or for worse is their problem. I hope for them to have only one family. I don't want them to have one wife then if they fight, to get a divorce and get another wife.

It appears that Angela's main concern is to have her children keep the tradition of respect and be successful in a marriage relationship. As she also expressed earlier, she has tried to keep the Mexican values alive in her family, but being in America has changed some of that. It has allowed her some luxury, but she has to deal with her children's assimilation into a foreign culture. Her role as a mother has also changed. Her role is not limited to taking care of the house like her mother. She is a working mother and has to make adjustments to keep up with her growing children. Despite this, her role is still best described as "crucial, not only because she works incessantly but also because she transmits to her children the religious beliefs, legends and customs that help preserve family and community life" (Riding, 1985). Angela is a strong-willed and loving parent. Her style of discipline is simple and springs from the foundation of respect.

Mexican-American Children

"We are just the same as you," was the response from Angela's older son when being asked about his cultural background. Maya and I explained that our histories were very different from one another. We let him know the intent of our study was to gain information so that we could come to better understand our students. He suggested that Maya and I tell him about ourselves, then. We agreed and began to chatter about our past, our family values, the differences in the roles people in our families played. He sat patiently listening to us, and when we were finished, he stood up and left to be with his friends. With a friendly gesture he said, "Well, I'll let these guys tell you everything," referring to his younger brother and three cousins.

We wondered how being a Mexican-American influences the perception of academic success, and what the Mexican-American children's goals were for the future.

Rosa's 17-year-old daughter, Martha, was talking about just wanting to find a job. It wasn't so important to her what she "became" as long as she had a good job. Martha presently does not want to go to college.

Sergio, age 7, doesn't like math or many other subjects in school. He doesn't like to study or do homework. However, he likes science because they do a lot of projects or experiments. He loves to dance. He says he wants to be a movie star in Hollywood. How long can he hold on to this image of who he *can* be? The fact that a high percentage of Mexican Americans drop out of school affirms the existence of factors, like poverty and acculturation, that increase the risk of academic failure. Mexican Americans have been noted to have the highest high school dropout rates in the United States (National Center for Educational Statistics, 1989).

In an investigation of the coping responses to psychosocial stressors among Mexican and Central American immigrants, the researchers, Padilla, Cervantes, Maldonado, and Garcia (1988) found that obtaining employment and other financial difficulties, language barriers, and acculturating to the lifestyle of the United States were the most stressful factors identified by both groups.

Educators and others relating to the lives of Mexican-American children need to understand the factors behind academic failure, and to be better prepared for adapting ways to approach the student and the student's needs. Some problems might not even be the academic challenge as much as the ability or desire to cope with the stress in the student's life that would make the academic experience less challenging. It would be a wrong assumption to think students experiencing academic failure want to be in that type of situation. A teacher's voice of encouragement is needed in order for them to develop their potential to the fullest extent.

Conclusion

The Gonzales family is not alone in their journey to be come a part of the United States. Millions have traveled a long distance in search of the "good life" here. Angela and her family are no different. Angela is no longer the homebound traditional Mexican wife. She works outside the home just like her husband and contributes equally to the family. She demands respect from her children as she manages to provide for them. She also realizes that acceptance in a small Midwest community is difficult, but tolerance and understanding have helped her to endure. Angela is not alone. Rosa has also faced similar obstacles. She has much to learn because she has only been here for such a short time. Of course, this journey is not only limited to the parents. The children have experienced difficulty, too, inside the walls of our schools.

Postscript From Judy Mehn

Working with people of other cultures is an opportunity to explore cultural differences, a challenge to present oneself respectfully without giving offense to their individual person or to their culture. Every individual has strengths and weaknesses, but to discover every individual's strengths, there is a need for acceptance and understanding of every culture. Although it is difficult, if not close to impossible for one individual to learn about and understand every culture, the *dialogic research project* presents an opportunity to gain a better understanding of a people that many misunderstand. We feel comfortable informing students about facts that we have learned through texts, and other literature sources about geographical areas and cultures that are to be studied. However, we would not feel justified interpreting any feelings or judging the actions of people from these pieces of literature, unless we have lived through their circumstances. The dialogic research gives insight that is taken directly from those who felt the blood race in their veins. The representation of their culture supplies a wealth of information that captures the images and motivates the reader or learner in a most involved manner.

My role as a *cultural storyteller* is to explore and relate the authentic experience to the students. The stories should not be interpreted by myself, but should be left open for interpretation by the students, with discussion so students can combine the knowledge of the information shared in the story with the interpretations of their peers. What a positive learning experience this can bring! Students will learn that stories are open to many interpretations, as well as discover a world behind each distinguishable culture. The idea is not to memorize details in order to pass a test and retain information to prove knowledgeable to others by recitation, the idea is to learn that there is always something to learn; there is always a story to be shared. The idea behind my philosophy of what a cultural storyteller should be is to understand that the important thing is to come to know the stories of others. If the occasion arises where there is disagreement between certain individuals, come to know their story, for with prevention of ignorance comes prevention of misinterpretation.

Many good things can come with the prevention of misinterpretation. Most obviously hate can dissolve to disagreement, or, at best, mutual understanding, and avoidance of what might otherwise become a hostile and violent situation. When misinterpretation is resolved, the role of the *cultural healer* may begin. To practice and exemplify what I teach to students is profoundly important, sharing my strengths and accepting my weaknesses, listening and reflecting on the words of others so I may grow as an individual and impress these values of knowledge and social acceptance onto the students. I find my role as a cultural healer is to guide students to a level of self-esteem and competency that will give them the power and ambition to discover who they are, who they can be, and what they want to do with their lives. My role as a teacher is to help others come to discover that success can be achieved not only as an adult, but as a child and youth as well, thinking of success as a lifestyle rather than a goal that is to be reached in the future. My role is to create and nourish opportunities where the students can come to know feelings of self-worth and acceptance of differences through a variety of learning experiences. These learning experiences include cooperative learning as well as individually collected knowledge, gaining a sense of independence along with the gift of learning how to work with others.

Along with developing a sense of self-worth in students comes the role of a *border crosser*. To develop self worth it is beneficial for the student to plunge into the depths of their own history, to discover the struggles and achievements that occurred in his or her past in order to appreciate and understand where they are at today. If students find that the actions of their ancestors have influenced their life, they might also realize how much of an impact they might have, or will be able to have, on their own future. A border crosser presents the opportunity for self- reflection as well as study of the social structure.

Sadly, Angela Gonzales and her family have moved out of the district, and we are no longer in contact with her. Yet, speaking with Angela Gonzales has helped me come to understand the types of problems she has had transitioning to life in America. I have listened to her story and contemplated ways that I would have wanted to help out to make life a little easier had I known her at that time. Although her role to me is one of a pioneer from whom I have much to learn, I also take from the events shared from her the chance to advance my role as a cultural boarder crosser. I have come to appreciate her hard work with long shifts and familial responsibilities. I recognize the devotion she has toward her family, which may have been misunderstood by me as a teacher who only had relations with the student at school and did not discover what circumstances she had endured to get to the place she is today. It will be easier for me to pause, question, and communicate with families instead of jump to conclusions of parental participation. Hearing her story of immigration took me to places I did not know even existed, but found out existed for many others. Listening to her plea for a more meaningful English learning experience, I am better able to adapt my teaching style to meet the needs of all students. What I do not take from her recommendations, I take from my own knowledge bank of ideas that arrived on contemplating her confrontations with learning English. By sharing her story with peers in my profession, I will be able to collect an even larger variety of material to use with students in the future. I hope all who learn of narrative study take advantage of this wonderful opportunity of shared experiences and have a positive learning outcome.

BEATRIZ AND JOHN: A BILINGUAL DIALOGUE JOURNAL

Mexican students are clear about what brings their families to Manitou Lake: It is the opportunity to work in the meat packing industry, an industry whose accompanying stench, unsanitary conditions, and abuse of immigrant workers has perhaps changed little since Sinclair first chronicled these details in *The Jungle* (1906). One of the high school bilingual teachers at Manitou Lake tells me that the packing companies knowingly entice undocumented workers to town, and when they have put in enough time to qualify for benefits, they are fired. If workers want, they can "start over." If they protest, their names can be given to the INS. Teresa, who has lived in Manitou Lake for 1 month, speaks of how this work affects her mother:

> *Mi mamá trabaja en el empacador. Es duro el trabajo. Llega muy cansada, y a veces llega con ampollas en las manos porque dice que es muy difícil, tiene que ser muy rápido. A una persona tener tanta rapidez y toda debería pagarle mas porque sufre más. Es un trabajo muy cansado.*
> [My mother works in the packing plant. The work is hard. She gets home really tired, and sometimes she has blisters on her hands because the work is very difficult, and she has to move very fast. For someone who has to work so fast they should pay more, because she suffers more. It is very exhausting work.]

I have followed the beginning (English) level bilingual students to their classes during the course of the school day in Manitou Lake. I have seen them helping each other in Economics class, while the teacher tells them to do their own work. I have seen them playing badminton in gym class, one of the few places where they are paired by their teacher with an English-speaking partner. I have seen them struggling with science exams about atomic structure, while their teacher, an experienced bilingual professional, appears frustrated with their low literacy, lack of knowledge of the concepts of science, and general unfamiliarity with the "rules" of U.S. school behavior. I have seen them previously with a bilingual language arts teacher who had first-hand experience with the lack of educational infrastructure in rural Mexico, and who created spaces for them to critically address their new lives in the United States; I see them now with his replacement, a well-meaning South American who has no teaching credentials, as she struggles with their growing complacency and resignation.

Yet, among those students who have not given up is Beatriz. Since she arrived last fall, she has embarked on a beautifully written dialogue journal with John, a poet, and student of TESOL at our university. Neither is literate in the language of the other. Nevertheless, with interpretation on both sides, they have found a way to understand each other. Below follow excerpts from their journal entries:

Hello John,

Trataré de escribirle en Inglés para contar le un poco de mi pueblo.
[I will try to write in English to tell a little bit about my town.] My town is small.
it is surrounded by mountain and between they pool of water.

Perdone que lla no le siga contestando en inglés pero es que se me hace muy
difícil y además tardaría mucho y el tiempo se está acavando.
[Sorry that I don't continue writing in English but it is very difficult for me and
besides it takes a lot of time and time is running out.]

En mi pueblo la mayoría son católicos y es por eso que creen en las imágenes
mi pueblo le dieron el nombre de S.S. Nicanandita por que ellos ablan una
lengua indigena llamado mixteco y Nicanandita en misteco es el lugar que
nace y frota el agua.
[In my town the majority are Catholics and because of this they believe in the
images. My town is called S.S. Nicanandita because the people their speak
an indigenous language called Mixtec and Nicanandita is Mixtec for the
place where the water springs forth.]

Pala otra le seguire contando mas. Hasta luego
[Next time I will tell you more. See you later.] … Béatriz

In his response, John contrasts the geography of his youth with that of
Beatriz' home town:

Beatriz, I was very happy to read your letter. I liked the part where you describe your home town. It sounds like paradise to me.

I can't remember if I told you where I was raised. I lived on the plains or llano
in Norte Dakota. It was flat and in some places you could see for 30 miles in
all directions. Sometimes, I miss that. I do like Wisconsin, too, but you can't
see very far here. I remember when I was on submarines—they go under-
water—in the navy, people would ask me about North Dakota. They wondered how I could live on the ship when I came from such a place.

I don't know if I will be able to write to you anymore because soon school
will end for me. But, I want to tell you how much I enjoyed writing to you....
Muchas gracias para escribir de me! Hasta luego o Buena suerte [Many
thanks for writing of me. See you later or good luck.]

John

John was trying to say goodbye, as he would be starting his clinical as-
signment in the spring and would no longer be in regular contact with me
and the journals. Beatriz, however, does not sense an ending to this correspondence, and she replies the following:

John,

Yo estoy muy contenta por que usted me sige contestando y además también estoy emocionada por que llega la navidad sabe esta navidad vaser la primera vez que la voy a pasar junto con mi papá por que las otra navidad mi papá a estado ausente del pueblo y es por eso que no estabamos juntos. yo espero que usted pase una feliz Navidad con su familia porque la navidad es muy bonito. Es un día lleno de amor, de alegría y sobre todo cuando esta toda la familia reunida, juntos con los amigos, ermanos. felicitandoce unos a otros
[I am very happy because you continue to write to me and besides I am excited about the arrival of Christmas. You know this is the first Christmas that I am going to spend together with my dad because the other Christmases my dad was gone from the village and so we couldn't be together. I hope that you have a Merry Christmas with your family because Christmas is very special. It is a day full of love, of happiness, and over all when all the family is reunited, together with friends, brothers and sisters, wishing each other well.]

Pero le confieso que auque estoy muy feliz por esta navidad también me ciento triste porque yo extraño a mis amigas. y es que nosotros cada año organisabamos una fiesta de jóvenes haciendo piñatas, intercambiamos regalos, juntas preparabamos todos para una fiesta y la pasabamos muy bien es por esa que yo las extraño.
[But I must confess that although I am very happy this Christmas I am also sad because I miss my friends. It is because every year we organize a party for the young people, making piñatas, exchanging gifts, we prepare everything for the party together and we have a great time, and because of this I miss them.]

Her journal reveals the reality that many Mexican immigrant students share with Beatriz: Often, one or both of their parents are separated from the family in Mexico, as they seek the means of economic survival in the United States. Yet her happiness at seeing her father again is tempered with a nostalgia for the celebrations with friends in her homeland. The poignancy of Beatriz' correspondence is heightened by this additional entry, before she hears from John again:

John,

yo estoy contenta por que yo ya podré escribirle denuevo yo estoy emocionada por que ya se acerca el verano para poder saler a pasear, ir a caminar. yo me diberti con la nieve por que ya esta primera vez que yo conocí la nieve. yo con mis hermanos fuimos a pasear cuando estaba nevando y nos dibertimos mucho jugando la nieve. yo quisiera saber como paso usted sus vacaciones, adonde fue, como paso la navidad.
[I am happy because I am able to write to you again. I am very excited about the approach of summer, to be able to get out and walk around. I enjoyed the snow because it is the first time I have experienced it. With my brothers and

sisters I went out when it was snowing and we really enjoyed playing with the snow. I would like to know how you spent your vacation, where you went, and what you did for Christmas.]

Toda mi familia estuvimos reunidos en mi casa e organizamos una comida tradicional del pueblo en de donde nosotros fuimos y todos la pasamos muy bonito yo espero que usted me conteste y me cuente de como paso la navida, es perare su contestación hasta luego John
[All of my family was together at my house and we made a traditional meal of my village and everything went very well. I hope that you will write to me and tell me how your Christmas was. I await your answer. See you later, John.] ...
Beatriz

When I meet John again and share these latest entries from Beatriz, he is very moved. He sits down in the lobby of our office and writes this response:

Beatriz,

It was so good to hear from you again! I know how you feel about friends that you miss. Many times I think about friends I have left behind and I am sad. I try to think about the fun we shared and this helps me to deal with my sadness. I sometimes imagine what they might be doing when I think of them, too.

All of your pleasant thoughts and wishes must have rubbed off on me over Christmas because I had a wonderful time with my family in Arizona. We had so many people that we had to stay in two different houses. Everyone took turns cooking and cleaning so that my Mom didn't have to do all of the work. On Christmas day, we exchanged some small presents and went to Mass. Father Alberto is the priest and he knows Spanish very well.

I am almost done with formal schooling. Soon, I will be a teacher. Even though I will be a teacher I will still be learning though. Education is very important throughout a person's life. I hope you continue to go to school for a long time because you are very smart! Don told me that you know three languages. It takes a lot of intelligence to do that. So, don't let anyone ever tell you that you are not smart....

I hope everything is going well for you, Beatriz. Soon, it will be spring and we will be able to see the trees and bushes budding. I am excited because then I can cook outside. Take care, Beatriz!

Peace,
John

It was quite evident how much these dialogue journals meant to students like Beatriz: They would look forward to my intermittent arrivals at their classroom, and eagerly attempt to decipher the messages sent by their friends at the university. Sadly, the students' wish to communicate on a regular basis with an English-speaking student was tested by the distance, and by the infrequency of the responses. Email dialogues would have been ideal, in that the students could have shared messages at any time. However, Manitou Lake West possesses only one computer with email access, and it is intended for the use of teachers, not students.

MEXICAN IMMIGRANTS: SUGGESTED READINGS AND WEB SITES

Byrd, B., & Byrd, S. M. (Eds.). (1996). The late great Mexican border: Reports from a disappearing line. El Paso, TX: Cinco Puntos Press.

Castaneda, J. (1995). *The Mexican shock: Its meaning for the United States*. New York: The New Press.

Davis, M. (1990). *Mexican voices, American dreams: An oral history of Mexican immigration to the United States*. New York: Henry Holt.

Dunn, T. (1996). *The militarization of the U.S.–Mexico border, 1978–1992: Low-intensity conflict doctrine comes home*. Austin, TX: CMAS Books.

Gutierrez, D. (1996). *Between two worlds: Mexican immigrants in the United States*. Wilmington, DE: Scholarly Resources.

Katzenberger, E. (Ed.). (1995). *First world, ha ha ha! The Zapatista challenge*. San Francisco: City Lights.

Maciel, D., & Herrera-Sobek, M. (Eds.). (1998). *Culture across borders: Mexican immigration and popular culture*. Tucson: University of Arizona Press.

Napolitano, V., & Solano, X. L. (Eds.). (1998). *Encuentros antropologicos: Power, identity and mobility in Mexican society*. London: Institute of Latin American Studies.

Oppenheimer, A. (1996). *Bordering on chaos: Guerrillas, stockbrokers, politicians, and Mexico's road to prosperity*. Boston: Little Brown.

Otero, G. (Ed.). (1996). *Neo-liberalism revisited: Economic restructuring and Mexico's political future*. Boulder: Westview Press.

Shadows of tender fury: The letters and communiques of Subcomandante Marcos and the Zapatista Army of National Liberation. New York: Monthly Review Press.

Web Sites

Building Chicana/o, Latina/o communities through networking. http://clnet.ucr.edu/research/educ.html

Center for Multilingual Muticultural Research. www.usc.edu/dept/education/CMMR/

Here is a sideways look at border crossing by Nancy Weaver from Bisbee, Arizona. http://www.themestream.com/articles/181946.html

Los ninos—helping children and families at the border. www.electriciti.com/~losninos/

Marcos, S. Comunicados de Subcomandante Insurgented Marcos. http://members.nbci.com/ezln1/comusep2.htm

Mexican history fills this site with an informative, easy-to-read time-line for reference. http://www.mexconnect.com/mex_/history.html

Red Mexicana de accion frente al libre comercio/The Mexican action network on free trade. NAFTA and the Mexican economy. http://www.igc.org/dgap/malecon.html

The National Clearinghouse for Bilingual Education. www.ncbe.gwu.edu/

The *Newspaper for Immigrants*—The newspaper for all immigrants and about immigration to America. http://www.immigrationnewsman.com/

San Francisco State University organization funds social, economic, political, and educational research. Check out papers and resources. http://www.sfsu.edu/~cecipp/

Urban minority families. eric-web.tc.columbia.edu/families/

Webspanol. www.geocites.com/Athens/Thebes/6177/

Willson, B. (2000). United States militarization of Mexico; unmasking the drug war; poverty and misery aggravation by NAFTA; militarization and repression in Mexico. http://www.globalexschange.org/campaigns/mexico/.slope

5

An Assyrian Family

REFUGEES FROM KURDISTAN

The Kurds have been referred to as the largest ethnic group never to have achieved statehood. They speak various dialects of Kurdish, a language related to Persian, and claim to be descended from the Medes, rulers of the ancient Persian empire. The vast majority of Kurds are practicing Muslims, with 80% being Sunni and 20% being Shi'ite. For centuries they have occupied the mountainous region that spans parts of Syria, Lebanon, Turkey, Iraq, Iran, and the former USSR. The population of Kurds in this region, which some call Kurdistan, is conservatively estimated at 16 million (McDowall, 1996).

In 1918, Kurdish leaders called for the establishment of an independent Kurdistan in this region. Although England and Turkey recognized Kurdistan as an independent state in the Treaty of Sevres in 1920, their nationhood remained unrecognized. When Kurds refused to recognize new political boundaries that divided their people between Turkey, Iraq, and other states, the British airforce in Iraq and the Turkish army in Turkey bombed and slaughtered them into submission. However, the new Iraqi state did allow Kurdish children to be educated in Kurdish, and made Arabic and Kurdish official languages within Iraqi Kurdistan (G. Simons, 1994).

Fighting between Kurdish nationalists and the various governments of the Kurdistan region has seldom ceased since the 1920s. At different times, British, Americans, Russians, Syrians, Iraqis, and Iranians have supported Kurds militarily to gain geopolitical advantage in the region, only to pull out support for Kurds when it became advantageous to do so. For example, the United States, Syria, and Iran actively supported Kurdish military attacks against Saddam Hussein's government in Iraq in the mid-1970s. However, when Iraq agreed to some concessions, Iran, troubled by its own Kurdish

Kurdish areas in Iraq and neighboring countries

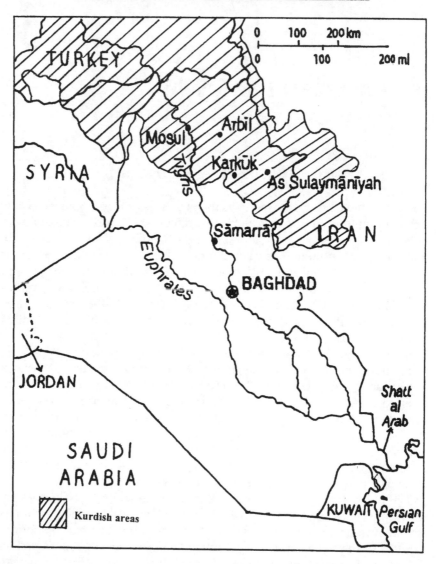

minority, pulled out its support, and the United States followed suit. Reinvigorated Iraqi forces decimated Kurdish resistance, causing some 20,000 casualties and 600,000 refugees (Brogan, 1989).

Additional thousands of Kurds became refugees during the 1980s, the period of the Iran–Iraq War. During this conflict, the United States, the Soviet Union, and various European nations helped to build up the Iraqi military arsenal, fearing a victory by the Ayatollah-led Iran. Iran recruited support once again from Iraqi Kurds. Iraq also utilized chemical weapons during the war, including its infamous attack on the Kurdish village of Halabja, which left 5,000 dead and 10,000 wounded. In the months following this massacre, the U.S. government refused to sanction Iraq, instead encouraging trade, issuing

> licenses for the delivery of biological products to the Iraqi Atomic Energy Agency, for the delivery of electronics equipment and machine tools to an Iraqi missile design center, a bomb plant, a missile factory, defence electronics factories, and a weapons manufacturing complex ... [The U.S. corporation] Bechtel secured a $1 billion deal to provide Iraq with a petrochemicals complex that the Iraqis intended to use in the production of mustard gas weapons, fuel-air explosives and rocket propellants. (Timmerman, 1992)

At the close of the Gulf War in 1991, President George Bush of the United States called on the Iraqi people to overthrow Saddam Hussein. Encouraged by the CIA and promised support from the United States, both Kurds in the north and Shi'ites in the south rebelled against Baghdad, only to be brutally put down by the Iraqi army on the ground while the United States maintained "no-fly zones" in the air. In the mid-1990s, the U.S. began to airlift the first groups of Kurdish refugees from Turkey, many whom had been on the U.S. payroll as part of plans to bring down Saddam Hussein's government. Thousands of other Kurds would seek asylum in the West in subsequent years. Those who have come to the United States find themselves in a country where they often don't know their neighbors, where there are relatively few Muslims, and where women often need to find a job (Gunter, 1999).

Katie Hinz came to know a family of refugees from Kurdistan during the fall of 1998 and has since maintained a relationship with them. They are distinct within the overall refugee group from Kurdistan, being Assyrian and non-Muslim, and they have faced their own persecution at the hands of their Muslim neighbors. Yet their stories of flight from their homeland and adjustment to life in the United States reflect many of the issues encountered by others from that area of the world, caught up in a geopolitical struggle where they are often considered expendable.

FIG. 5.1.   Dunya (second from left) dances with friends at the 1999 New Year's celebration.

FIG. 5.2.   Dunya (far left) poses with two friends at the Kurdish New Year celebration, the first day of spring, 1999.

FIG. 5.3.   The Dawoods dance at the 1999 New Year celebration.

FIG. 5.4.   Left to right: Mahira, Sarjon, Dunya, and Mahir, November 1999.

FIG. 5.5. Sarjon, Dunya, and Lark, Menominee Park, Oshkosh, Wisconsin, spring 1999.

FIG. 5.6. Left to right: Katie Hinz, Mahira Dawood, and Hushniya Dawood at the Oshkosh Opera House where Mahira is part of the chorus for "Camelot," spring 2001.

FIG. 5.7. Hushniya and Katie Hinz, Oshkosh North High School, December 1998.

FIG. 5.8. Hushniya and Mahira, Menominee Park, Oshkosh, Wisconsin, spring 1999.

— THE DAWOOD FAMILY —

Katie Hinz
With the Dawoods

A strange language was swirling around me, and paranoid thoughts were
running through my mind. Are they talking about me? Is my face as red as
it feels? Scanning the spacious living room, I noticed that everyone had
taken their shoes off. I didn't want to get off on the wrong foot, but my
Nikes were tapping nervously on their mauve carpet. I was on the outside
looking in, feeling very uncomfortable. Everything from the Arabic television station to the peculiar smelling food was comfortable to them and new
to me. They were very polite and nice and offered me tea. I hate tea, but
in the Dawoods' house I wanted to fit in so I did as the Dawoods do. Many
visits later, the tea and language largely spoken remain the same, but I no
longer worry and just go with the flow. They have made me feel at home,
encouraging me to come over and telling me not to worry when I appear
uncomfortable. For Sarjon (23), Munir (21), Samir (19), Hushniya (18),
Mahir (17), and Mahira (15), the experience of feeling out of place has
been repeated many times in Iraq and in the United States, but uncondi-
tional acceptance has not.

These six siblings, along with Sarjon's wife Dunya (21) and son Lark (4),
were among 53 Kurdish refugees from Iraq brought to Oshkosh in 1997.
They are all here to escape the oppressive Baath regime of Saddam Hussein.
But, for the Dawoods and other Assyrians, their Kurdish neighbors and government often added to their hardships.

> The Dawoods life has been a roller coaster ride
> of highs, lows
> and unexpected turns.
> Through it all they have tried
> to live in peace,
> with whomever their neighbors may be.

Historical Perspective

Out of 20 million Iraqis, less than 1 million are Christians (Impressions from
Iraq, 1999). Many Christians trace their ancestry back to the Assyrians, the
builders of the great Mesopotamian civilizations, which collapsed around
605 B.C. (The Assyrians, 1999).

The ancestry of the Kurds is also clothed in controversy and uncertainty. Historians trace their descendants back to the Medes, an Indo-European tribe that descended from Central Asia into the Iranian plateau around 614 B.C., emerging as one of the primary pre-Islamic dynasties. After the Arab conquest in the 7th century, the term *Kurd* was used to refer to many other ethnic and tribal groups who had intermingled, created new communities, and also lived in the Zagros mountain ranges of northwestern Iran. The assimilation genetically, culturally, socially, and linguistically of these various mountain people marked the birth of Kurdish autonomy in the 7th century (Entesser, 1992).

The Assyrians most recent chance for self-government was after World War I when they were promised their own country by the British, in part for their valiant efforts in fighting the Ottoman Empire. They agreed to Britain's offer of the Mosul district in Northern Iraq, which lies across the Tigris River from the ancient Assyrian capital of Nineveh (The Assyrians, 1999). This arrangement was never honored by the British.

The Kurds were also promised statehood after World War I, in 1920. This proposal by President Wilson of the United States was vetoed by Great Britain and France after oil was discovered in the Iraqi Kurdistan region (Efty, 1996). Ever since, the Kurds in Iraq have struggled for rights and autonomy.

The Iraqi government's policy of Arabization in the 1970s and 1980s and more subtle forms ever since has made ethnicity a factor in all areas of life (Entesser, 1992). Lack of a united political movement, influential constituents, and small numbers are factors that have allowed the Assyrians' voice to remain unheard (Hanna, 1998). During this period, the Baath government intentionally denied the existence of Assyrians, categorizing them as Kurdish or Arab Christians (Hanna, 1998). Recently the Iraqi government has made efforts to support Christians but still maintain that they are Arabs (UNHCR [United Nations High Commission for Refugees], 1996).

Sarjon doesn't understand why everyone from his Kurdish friends to the government, believe that the Assyrian culture does not exist: "We have our own language, traditions, and church (Chaldean Catholic). We have no country, but our flag (Assyrian) will always mean my culture. American flag means my country, but I will always be Assyrian, too." Kurds comprise 15% of Iraq's population and are the majority in a 74,000 square kilometer area in northern Iraq, which was once part of the region known as Kurdistan (Ghassemlou, 1980). Recently, separatist efforts by the PUK (Union of Kurdistan) and PKK (Kurdistan Democratic Party) and severe human rights violations by Hussein pushed this demand into the international spotlight. In 1992, the United States helped secure a 36,000 square kilometer region in Northern Iraq and instituted a Kurdish government (UNPO [Unrepresented Nations and Peoples Organization], 1999).

Although Assyrians and Kurds share a common homeland and have been subjected to some of the same oppressive Iraqi government policies, they often direct anger against each other. Main sources of friction between Kurds and Assyrians are property claims, religion, and political affiliation (Cases of Kurdish Attacks, 1999). Sarjon believes his Kurdish neighbors "wanted us to leave because they don't like us, our church, our language, nothing." Sarjon's observation are supported by the apparent toleration and condoning of crimes against Assyrians in Dohuk and other cities in the Kurdish governed region (Cases of Kurdish Attacks, 1999). Thus, the Dawoods' Assyrian heritage and Chaldean Catholic faith has influenced their relationships, quality of life, and treatment by both governments, and by both Arabs and Kurds. Maintaining the Assyrian language, faith, and practices, and adding those of Kurds and Arabs to get by was their reality.

On the Move

On July 1, 1975, Toma and Kiliaya Dawood gave birth to the first of six children, Sarjon. They began raising him in a one room house in a small Kurdish village in Northern Iraq. His parents dreamed of raising a family here, near the mountains amidst the countryside dotted with a few other homes. Sarjon can't remember this village, but has heard the story: "The government said we had to move into a town. I don't know why they make everyone leave. From there we move to Mosul." Iraq had just signed the Algers treaty with Iran, which agreed to stop supporting the Kurdish revolt. As a result, the Iraqi government vied for control by attacking villages and resettling Kurds into cities where their activities could be monitored (Graham-Brown, 1995).

Munir, Samir, and Hushniya were born while the family lived in Mosul. Sarjon remembers then it was time to move again: "In 1980 when the war started with Iran, my dad said, 'Let's move north again' and we come to Zakho. We stayed for 17 years, until we come here." Zakho, a city of 2500 people, mainly Kurds, is where they all grew up and the place they call home.

> I have never feared having to move,
> from the only house I have ever known
> Because the government doesn't approve.
> Or been caught
> in the webs woven by others
> So that all of my planning was for naught.

Zakho

Snow-topped mountains loomed above this city of narrow, red dirt streets lined with stone houses. Wooden shambles for those who are poor are scattered on the outskirts of town. Small shops sell food and goods outside on the sidewalk. Nothing conceals the beautiful view of the Zagros mountains and the only notable building in town is the hospital.

Toma Dawood picked a beautiful city in which to raise his children. With Mahira on the way, they would soon be a family of eight. His daughters and wife became attached to a church that had a rich tradition of Chaldean Catholic faith. His sons grew up enjoying hunting wild pigs in the mountains. Mahir's favorite thing to do on hot days was to swim in the Tigris River. "It was so clean, it was blue. We swim across and are in a different city. Here, I never swim in the river because it's brown."

Sarjon wishes his father could have gotten to know Zakho and watched his children grow up:

> Just after we moved he had to go to war (1981). He came back to see us for 7 to 10 days every 35–40 days, but he always go back. It's not like here in America where it's volunteer. In our country we don't have this. When you're 18 you have to go to the army unless you're in school. This is why I was 8 when my dad died fighting for our country.

> The government gave them money,
> promised them cultural and religious rights,
> appointed a few Assyrians to government positions.
>> But they imprisoned Sarjon,
>> neglected their promises,
>> threatened their lives.
> Some Kurds were their best friends;
> two lived in their home.
>> Others broke their windows,
>> harassed them,
>> stole from them,
>> and killed their mother.

Compensation

You can't put a price on a life or make up for taking a father away. But Sarjon is grateful to the Iraqi government for easing the monetary strain that life without their only breadwinner would have caused:

> The government paid for us to build a house. We started a one story house. My mom wasn't working at that time and I could just go to school and not work because they were also paying us $150 a month. We could also choose a car or more

money. We took money because our family was small, and there was no one to drive the car. Women don't drive there, not too many, even less in the north by us. Later, we ask for more money and we built another story.

This two-story stone house with two bedrooms, a kitchen, and living room on each floor became their home. Mahir remembers their middle-class neighborhood with a nice sidewalk, wider than the ones lining their city street here. They rented the upstairs to a Kurdish teacher and her sister. Munir and Sarjon shared a room and mom slept in the big room with the rest of the kids. Munir joined them after Sarjon and Dunya were married. In the summer everyone slept on top of their roof. They had a washer, dryer, refrigerator, freezer, and gas stove which are some of the same comforts that I grew up with in my middle-class home.

> I sit and dream I was there,
> sleeping on top of their roof at night,
> breathing and feeling the fresh cool air,
> filtering in through the meshy net
> that keeps bugs
> from biting my head.
> Feeling safe on my metal bed,
> with everyone else on their roofs nearby,
> gazing up at comets and constellations in the sky.

Expression

I have always taken language for granted. When I think of who I am, I never think of *English speaker*. But English words and expressions are what define me in my mind. For the Dawoods, learning another language was a necessity to get into school, go to the store, or understand anything at all. They couldn't use the language that they dream in, because in Iraq not all languages are treated equally. Assyrian language derives from the Aramaic language spoken in much of the Middle East in Biblical times (Assyria, 1999). Iraq prefers to keep Assyrian out of the present. Although they were prohibited from public use of the Assyrian language, Assyrians always spoke Assyrian at home. They grew up speaking Assyrian, Arabic, and Baba Kurdi (a Kurdish dialect), forming a vocabulary that is a mosaic of these different languages. For Sarjon, they all blend together fluidly. At home Sarjon often throws in words from each of these to get across his picture:

> If I am with Arabic people I speak Arabic, with Kurdish, Kurdish, and with our people, Assyrian. When I started school it was all Arabic— Arabic—that's why I never

forget it. Now, I can only write Arabic. I didn't like Kurdish too much so that's why I can't write it or read it a lot. I do feel bad that I don't know how to write our language [Assyrian]. Munir knew some but he forgot, too. Most Assyrians don't know how to read and write it. There is nothing written in our language, the government won't let us. So everyone just forgets or never learns.

Kurdish people don't know how to speak our language; maybe it's too hard for them. But, our language is the easiest in the world to learn. But, nobody tries—not Kurds, not Arabs—but I'll teach you.

Faith

The Dawoods are members of the largest Christian community in Iraq, the Chaldean church, which numbers 600,000 (Impressions of Iraq, 1999). Despite efforts by both Muslim governments (Iraqi and Kurdish) to limit worship and fragment parishes, the Dawoods remained committed to their church.

Dunya mentioned a decline in the Assyrian population in Zakho and her hometown of Dohuk, which is about 30 miles away:

> There are not a lot of Assyrians in the North anymore. Most move south into Baghdad because the Kurds fight all of the time and don't like us. They are jealous of us because now Saddam likes us better. He has Assyrians guard his house and some are in the government (e.g., Tariq Azziz). I have family in Holland and Greece and others leave, too.

The appointment of Christians to senior positions in the government and the Baath Party, and restoration of churches and monasteries were likely in exchange for the Assyrians loyalty and silence (Hanna, 1998). Evidence of Hussein's recent efforts to befriend Assyrians is the large number (30) of Chaldean parishes that have sprung up in Baghdad (Assyria: The Catholic Encyclopedia, 1999). Still, the Dawoods kept attending their small church, which was guarded at night, and fixed their broken windows and doorbell, which were routinely targeted on Christmas and Easter.

Hushniya never worried about her neighbors animosity toward Christians. She enjoyed church, hummed hymns, and loved signs of her faith:

> We had rosaries, pictures of Jesus, and crosses in our house. Assyrians with cars have rosaries and crosses hanging from the mirror like my brother does here. My mom went to church every day when I was little, and we all went on Sunday. When we were young, we went to class at church. They teach us about the Bible, and church, it was so cool. Teachers were all nice.

> We wore nice clothes and a scarf over our head. At the altar we had a picture of Jesus, the girls sit behind boys, women behind men, and old women behind old men. On Sundays you can't eat until after church. Holy days we go to church too. Easter is my favorite. We have party at church and dress really nice. For 40 days before Easter, my mom didn't eat meat and we didn't on Friday. We cover all of the crosses in our house. On Easter we sing and dance, it's so nice.

I consider myself a good Catholic. I go to church most Sundays, try not to eat meat on Fridays during Lent, enjoy Christmas presents and Easter baskets, and have a small cross above my bed. Three-hour masses, church every day, dressing up for church and sitting behind guys, and 40 days without meat might challenge my faith. Would I want to go to church if there were guards outside to protect it, or just turn and walk away? But trying times cemented the Dawoods' beliefs, instead of leading them to ask, why doesn't God do something?

Fun

Many of the Dawoods' best memories of Iraq are of parties and picnics. The first day of spring is a traditional party day and everything stops. Their whole town gathers and crosses the bridge from one side of the Tigris River to the other. Dancing and singing were the main attractions for Sarjon:

> We dance a lot because that's all we have. The government takes a lot away, or we have no money to do other things. Christmas and Easter are our big parties for just us. We do our [Assyrian] dances then. They are different from Kurdish dances. We move our feet different, and wear different clothes.

> I got a taste of this excitement at the transplanted version
> of this event at an area park.
> The weather was too cold,
> there was no bridge,
> but the dancing, food, and friendly atmosphere
> proved to me that their parties
> are better than the ones we have here.
> I tried to dance and follow the human chain's
> fluid rhythm circling around and around,
> but I was tapping when they were hopping.
> I wished I could fade into the ground,
> but their support kept me from stopping.

War

From April 1987 to April 1988, the Iraqi government launched campaigns of chemical warfare (mustard, nerve, and cyanide gases) on seven cities in the

Iraqi Kurdistan region (Gunter, 1992). This campaign, considered genocide by many, resulted in killing 100,000 and forcing 800,000 people to flee (Gunter, 1992). The worst attack occurred in March, 1988, in the town of Halabja. Sarjon remembers that this was the talk around Zakho: "They throw chemicals on a city, they kill 5,000. I hear they only leave one man. But, they never throw chemicals on our city. They never can, because we're too close to Turkey (4 miles away). Otherwise maybe we be dead."

On August 2, 1990, Iraq launched an invasion of Kuwait. Saddam Hussein's refusal to withdraw from Kuwait prompted the United States and allies to launch Operation Desert Storm on January 16, 1991 (Hilsman, 1992). By mid-February, I was glued to the TV. I was especially interested because my 6th-grade teacher was there with an army reserve unit. He promised that he would be back in time to be our softball coach.

Meanwhile, 6,000 miles away, Sarjon was watching the story unfold in his own backyard. The war efforts were concentrated in the south, 700 miles from Zakho. The war prompted Sarjon to attempt to leave the country at 16 years of age.

Sarjon's Story

Some people run to Turkey, and from there go to different countries. I was one of these people coming out running from my country. I didn't like it there. School was hard, teachers were mean, the people and government weren't nice. I wanted to be free of this. I knew I could make a better life. I planned to study in Turkey or maybe to come to the United States someday.

Me, my cousin, and four friends left on February 21, 1991, to try to go to Turkey. We go by car, like here you might say taxi, through the west side of our city. We drive for an hour. At 8 or 9 at night we start walking through mountains. We walk until 7 in the morning. We only have to get past the last mountain and then we are in Turkey. We were so close, but not lucky. The Iraqi military catch us and bring us from the mountains to jail.

The first day they ask us questions and want us to answer what we were doing. Of course at first we didn't say, but then they hurt us with cables or wood. It was very, very bad. They hit me with a cable—my back, my butt, my foot. After that they put me in a small room. They tie my hands and feet and put electrodes on my tongue and turn on. Then I tell the truth. Some other people die, they hurt them so much.

We stay one night in jail in the north, then they move us south to Irbil where we stay 9 days. Then they move us to Mosul for 15 days, and then to Dohuk, but we just stay there a few hours. Then they move us to Sulayminah, because there was nobody to bring us back to jail in south because they were all fighting the Kurds. We stayed there for a second day and they were still fighting. Then the Kurdish government broke the door and we came out.

Of course I went back to my family in Zahko, it was about 20 miles from where I was. I go home and nobody thought I would ever be back. I just knock on the door and my mom says "Whaaaaaaa." It was like a surprise for everybody.

When I came back there was no school, no nothing. In late March, Iraqi [troops] came back north again and people started running from their homes. We run to mountains, too. I was scared a lot because if they caught me again they would kill me. My mom said, we don't have to go, that we can stay at home because the kids are small. I told them, no, I have to go, so I went with my grandma and uncle.

On the second day in the mountains I thought a lot about them and thought about what might happen to them. That if the government came, maybe they kill them. I went home again to take all of them with me. But nobody was home.

Flight and Return

Hushniya remembers her family's frantic flight when the Iraqi offensive intensified: "We were not going, but then bullets came through our door, and they put gasoline or something on my mother's leg and burned it. Our neighborhood all tried to leave. We went in a big truck, there was like 10 or 20 families, to the mountains in Turkey."

Sarjon was still searching for them; hoping for the best, fearing the worst: "I looked all around the mountains to see where they were, but I didn't see them. We were all in Turkey but they went a different way."

Reprisals in the north left an estimated 468,000 Kurds along the Iraq–Turkey border; the chances of a family reunion were slim, whereas the odds of misfortune were high (Gunter, 1992). Relief reports estimated as many as 1,000 were dying every day from the bitterly cold conditions and disease (Graham-Brown, 1995). Sarjon reports:

We had blankets and put them together kind of like a tent. We made fire with wood, but it was very cold and there was a lot of snow. Sometimes I stand in snow. It was so high you couldn't see me. No one was helping us, but we met other family. There was some food but not enough, we were cold, sick, and hungry all the time.

Hushniya and the rest of the family were relying on the temporary camps set up by coalition forces:

We were in tents, and they gave us bread and chicken, but we had to walk to get water. We found a teacher from our church and we stay with her. It was cold and rainy, but it was good there, because I wasn't scared. You could see people and walk and play. But my mom said, "You two are girls; you stay with me." But, for Easter she sewed me and Mahira the same clothes, so we felt happy.

On April 18, 1991, Iraq and the United Nations signed an agreement allowing nongovernmental organizations (NGOs) to assume relief operations (Gunter, 1992). The United States protected this arrangement by threatening to attack if any Iraqi aircraft flew past the 36th parallel into the no-fly zone (Graham-Brown, 1995). The military presence of American and British troops in the safe haven area and along the Turkey barrier backed up this threat.

Although the rest of the family remained among the estimated 180,000 Kurds still in Turkey, Sarjon returned home.

For a month and a half I was home alone. My family sent me a letter saying that they were in Turkey and from there they were going to Australia. I felt really sad because I thought I never [would] see them again. I thought I would just stay at home and if they came maybe I would go with them. They were too far from me and I couldn't go back there again. I had no car so I would need to walk maybe 3 to 4 days and it would be very dangerous. Especially in the mountains because if you don't have any gun, an animal can kill you or other people might think you are an animal and they [might] kill you. But, one day (in June) I went shopping and when I came home they were back. I say what you are doing here, and I was very, very happy to see them.

Hushniya was also surprised with their sudden change of plans to come home:

My uncle sent a letter telling my mother she had to come back. We have our house and Sarjon was there. So we walk back, it was a long way, I can't remember how far. When I came home I took a bath for 3 hours. There was no water to shower (in the mountains), and my body was so dirty. I was so tired because I didn't sleep at all that day, just walk. I was so, so happy to be home.

Life Under Operation Provide Comfort

Zakho became the military coordination center for a four nation (United States, Turkey, French, and British) force responsible for monitoring and reporting on the stability of the relief efforts of Operation Provide Comfort (OPC) in the 14,600 square mile zone in northern Iraq (Ritchie, 1996). Home was safe again, but nothing was back to normal. Schools were still closed, many houses were destroyed, and almost everyone was unemployed. Sarjon remembers the process of getting life back in order:

> At first we [were] just happy to be home and safe. The United States helped set up a government to protect Kurdish people. Organizations came and they set up hospitals, and built people houses. If you need help, they help, the army brought food and gave to all people. We take food every month.

> Then in June (1991), I met my teacher at the store and he asked why I don't come to school. I say no, I don't like it, nobody likes it. Every year it gets harder. He said I only have 1 year left then I graduate, and can go onto to college. I said it's a good idea, so I got done with high school and I go to tech school. After that I didn't like it any more so I quit in 1993.

Mahir and Mahira also returned to school. Hushniya and Samir were not enjoying academic success before the war. Both were stuck in the lower grades and wanted to quit. Neither returned to school after returning from the mountains. Hushniya helped her mother at home and cleaned houses. Samir and Munir shined shoes and sold produce from the family's garden.

Death in the Family

Sarjon married Dunya during this time. The Dawood family embraced Dunya, and Sarjon and Dunya were awaiting the arrival of a child. Hushniya remembers that her mom was happy. Although they were all working just to get by, the sacrifices seemed worth it. Kiliaya worked from 11 a.m. 5 p.m. with an American relief organization. Dunya worked all day at Shelter Now, and Sarjon was a delivery man from 8 a.m. to 4 p.m. Kiliaya was looking forward to seeing her first grandson.

Sarjon's eyes and face still show pain and hate when he retells this tale: "Mom was walking home from work, and she got shot. My aunt was with her but she could do nothing, she died fast. Nobody did anything. The [Kurdish] government said it was an accident. Nothing happened, she was just dead and we buried her at church."

No one has claimed responsibility for their mother's death. It is just another innocent life, adding to the long line of Assyrians killed in Kurdistan. The killing of Assyrian Patriarch Mar Benyamin Shimun on March 3, 1918, had precipitated a mass migration of Assyrians out of the region. Shimun went to assure Kurdish leaders that his followers would remain living as peaceful semi-independent people in the Itakkari Mountains in Turkey. From inside the house he saw troops on roofs surrounding them. As he was leaving his meeting with the Kurdish chief, hundreds of Kurds opened fire, outnumbering him and his bodyguards. It is said that only six of his companions escaped. The Assyrians could not fight back and were forced to flee into the Urmia and Salamas districts in Iran, no longer safe (Genocides Against the Assyrian Nation, 1999).

Kiliaya Dawood had insisted on going to work and raising her family in their home, despite the flight of many fellow Assyrians and family members. She, too, saw signs that the Kurdish government was aiming to drive out Assyrians, and that the Iraqi government was not pleased with American relief operations. It was safe and OK, she told her family, making them feel secure and at peace. Samir remembers her advice: "Do not fight when people are bad to us. I never start a fight, but sometimes you have to fight."

Her death was not an ambush meticulously planned, but one bullet produced the same effect. Her six children were left without their matriarch, the only parent they had left. There was no army chasing after them, but the only security they had left was shattered. Even 10 year old Mahira couldn't be sheltered from the loss: "I couldn't believe it at first. It was like I didn't know what happened, when I see her body I thought she was sleeping. Nobody told me, but everyone was crying. Then I knew. I couldn't eat or sleep, I just felt sick."

Mahira thinks about "what-ifs" every time she misses her mom:

> I wish we went to Australia. Then my mom would be alive and everything would be just like always. I never want to forget her face. She was my best best friend. Now my heart is in a thousand pieces. Our house is empty without her voice, her laugh, her stories. I think about her every day all the time.

There was nothing to do but go on with life. Lark, Sarjon and Dunya's child, entered the world a few months later. Instead of spending her days learning from her mother, Hushniya was on her own, caring for Lark during the day while everyone else worked and or went to school.

When I was 11 I was completing fifth grade. I was learning that I was responsible for handing in papers on time, not forgetting my books, and remembering my locker combination. Hushniya was responsible for making sure Lark was safe and not crying, cleaning the house, and cooking meals. If I wasn't responsible, I missed recess. If Hushniya messed up the whole family paid the price. She learned fast to pick up where her mother left off. The house was clean, her mom's recipes tasted authentic, but it wasn't the same without her (mother) laugh, her smiles, her stories.

Shattered Security

In September 1996, Kurdish Democratic Party (KDP) forces backed by Iraqi troops took control of areas that were under Kurdish autonomy (Hirst, 1996). This strategic reversal was a public relations nightmare for President Clinton, who was claiming victory for stabilizing the Kurdish situation by protecting the area and helping establish a Kurdish government. The United States launched cruise missiles on sites in southern Iraq in retaliation for this Iraqi offensive.

The Dawoods had much more at stake than their reputation and future employment possibilities. Again Sarjon was waiting for Hussein to dictate the family's next move. He remembers listening to the radio: "We hear Saddam say, 'I'm going to take over the north again. And that any Iraqi people who work with American organizations I'm going to arrest them and kill them.'"

Allied military and OPC personnel began evacuating Zakho and heading to Silopi, Turkey (Allied Base in North Iraq Moved, 1996). Dunya's job was gone, and her family was on the Iraqi military's hit list. Now they would need to run from the military that their father had served in, directed by the government that had helped them build their home.

In November, the United States decided to evacuate employees and their families of U.S. funded NGOs, including Shelter Now International (McCormick & Pounds, 1997). Sarjon didn't care about the process behind receiving his papers, he was just relieved they finally came:

> Three months after everyone left, Shelter Now sent a fax to our city and our names were on the paper so we can pass. They send them to Turkey's government so they had our name so we could pass.

> We only took some clothes. I gave our house to our uncle, just in case we ever go back. Then we don't have to buy one. We sell some furniture and leave everything else with them.

> Americans helped us get to southern Turkey. They give us food, and we slept outside in tents for 2 days. First we were in Silopi, then Batman. From there we moved by American airplane to Guam.

The Dawoods arrived in Guam jet-lagged, but safe. There they got a taste of English but with 4,500 other Kurds there, learning English wasn't a priority. It was a much needed chance to relax. They had enough to eat, and could walk around freely. Sarjon was finally sure that they wouldn't be back surprising their uncle:

> We stayed 3 months, 12 days in Guam at Camp Anderson [waiting for asylum papers to be processed]. If you had a sponsor, they brought you to America. We go

around the camp, watching cinema, playing soccer, volleyball, basketball, and ping pong. The weather was nice for us. We didn't get a typhoon when we were there but the people that came before us, they got a typhoon.

> The Dawoods were ready to find a home,
> to go to bed knowing they would not have to leave again.
> Finally the day came to leave behind Guam.

> From the palms of Hawaii,
> to sunny San Francisco;
> across Chicago's massive sky scape,
> landing in Appleton.
> A short drive later they were in Oshkosh.
> Relieved to finally stop and not move
> to another city anytime soon.

American Firsts

For the Dawoods coming to Oshkosh meant starting over in everything and learning a new way of life. "It's difficult for us. Everything is strange, everything is new, and we cannot speak the language," Sarjon was quoted as saying in the *Oshkosh Northwestern* newspaper, on his arrival (Ebert, 1997, p. A1). Greeting them at the runway in Appleton was a host family who would help them get used to their new surroundings. A network of resources assembled by the church that sponsored them helped them learn the language, find jobs, and get comfortable.

Mahira's biggest concern was making friends and fitting in at school: "When we first came I was scared. I barely knew any English. At school I was so embarrassed, I couldn't understand anything. There was a translator [Kurdish] but I felt so stupid."

Here everything was strange: American societal norms, accepted practices, and laws put a different spin on life. Driving was one of the first things Sarjon and Dunya set out to learn. I also remember learning to drive which was essential for the growth of my social life. I dreaded driving because I didn't feel at ease, which I blame for the failure of my first driving test. Sarjon and Dunya not only had no idea how to drive, but they had not been backseat drivers, getting to see how Americans drive. My dad complains that driving in Chicago is a whole different game. But, at least the rules are the same. Sarjon and Dunya didn't drive in Iraq but they knew that their rules weren't like ours. In Iraq, there is no speed limit, and not much to worry about except for a few stop signs.

After months of taking in our rules, they both got their licenses. Dunya got into two accidents within 3 months after getting her license, just like I did after I got mine. Our first accidents were both minor fender benders. I pulled out and hit a car, and she backed into another car. But, it was just bad timing, because if those other cars wouldn't have been there, our records would both be clean.

Our second accidents were also similar; we both got hit going through green lights, and in both cases our assailant took off and was caught. This time my dad blamed me for not watching out for ignorant drivers. Dunya was afraid to call the police, thinking it was somehow her fault, and my dad debated calling the police figuring that the driver who hit me wouldn't get caught. Luckily the police came through for both of us and our records have been clean ever since.

Two years later the initial uncertainty and anxiety that Sarjon and Dunya felt toward driving, shopping, working, balancing their checkbook, and many other American experiences have been erased. Sarjon is content with his job as a machine operator at Oshkosh Coil Spring, and Dunya and Munir are happy to have found full-time day jobs packaging meat at Silver Creek Meat. In the fall of 1998, the family moved out of the home that the church had rented for them. They are pooling their money to afford a four bedroom house, furniture, three cars, food, and other essentials. To Sarjon this is a good start: "Here we all have jobs, we keep working hard. We will have enough money for all life. People are nice here. We are free and safe. Nobody kills us and schools are good for my son."

Love and Marriage

There are many contrasts between dating and marriage in Kurdistan and the United States. Sarjon remembers one of the girls he knew in Iraq: "I love a girl, [she is] not my girlfriend, but I like her and she likes me. I want to marry her. There is no dating. I just see her at school or outside. Nobody can know just me and her, if anybody knows, whoa, it's a big, big problem."

A year after getting used to school and English in the United States, Mahira was thinking about boys. She is caught between what she has seen in Iraq and what life is like here. "Back home nobody had a boyfriend. It was just a group of girls. If you did, it had to be a secret. You could only see them at night when everyone else is sleeping. Here everybody has boyfriends."

When I was in high school, my mom would ask who's with who today, knowing that it would change tomorrow. This is the opposite of Sarjon's experience, where it was so hard to get to know one girl and very secretive. Naturally, he is very protective of his sisters, and doesn't encourage them to date. Mahira knows if she had a boyfriend and Sarjon found out, there would be big problems: "If he knew we were with boyfriends he wouldn't let us go. He thinks we're too young because in Iraq it's not like here. You only date if it's OK with your family. It's not OK with him so we shouldn't."

Marriage in Iraq and in the United States is also quite different. My dad is lucky that all he had to do was get down on one knee, and risk rejection from my mom. Following traditional custom, Sarjon first asked his family if they would let him marry the girl he loved. Kiliaya trusted her son's judgment and went to the girl's family to get their consent. Unfortunately for Sarjon, her family didn't trust their daughter or him: "Her mom didn't like me and told my family, 'I never give my daughter to you.' "

Sarjon was very disappointed and not ready to risk rejection again. But he couldn't stop thinking about Dunya, a girl he had seen in the mountains: "I first saw my wife when I was in the mountains in 1991. I thought she was pretty, but then I [did] not see her and fell in love with that other girl. I remembered her though, and I was lucky she was my relative. Her mom and my mom were second cousins so I got to meet her again."

Dunya remembers, "I liked him right away, and I said, I want to marry him some day."

Hushniya excitedly followed the wedding plans:

We really liked Dunya so much so we all went to her family and asked them. They said yes! We needed to pay a lot of money, but this is how it always is. My mom started working for an American organization to help pay. She cleaned and did everything, she was so good and fast. Sarjon worked too, and we paid Dunya's family for the wedding. We had to pay for the singer, so we borrowed money and had to pay [it] back.

February 13, 1993, was a cold and windy day. This was not what Hushniya imagined as perfect weather for an outdoor wedding in the street and on their roof:

Sarjon ate burnt rice. It's bad luck. It snowed, it never snows. My mom wanted to go to this place where there's lots of dances, because it was so cold. But our house was big, so my uncle said we should stay and have it inside. We say OK, because then we didn't need to pay [for the room], but we were kind of mad.

My aunt send me a dress from Baghdad, because I didn't have one. We fixed it and made it really pretty. Everyone told me, "you look so good in that dress!" Sarjon wore his blue suit, and Dunya her blue dress tie that they always wore to church. Their wedding wasn't as nice as my uncle's, and some of our friends. They were too young (Dunya was only 15 and Sarjon was 18). We had big circle [dance]; some kids, some old people, it was so fun. Me and Mahira were jumping and laughing because we were so happy.

You party one or two days. We did two days, and the second day we all were still singing. I wore a white sweatshirt and blue jeans and makeup. Everyone asked,

"Who's that girl?" Nobody knew me because I made up my face and fixed my hair, so pretty.

The perfect marriage full of excitement dances through my mind sometimes. A really nice, handsome, smart, and faithful guy will suffice. Mahira hopes for the same, but she hesitates to consider an American:

I never marry an American because he probably [would] divorce me. In Iraq I didn't know anybody who was divorced. Here I already know lots. At our weddings, Father always says, you are together forever. Don't they say that here? Why don't people listen?

At school, some girls are pregnant. They are too young and not even married. That's not how it is in Iraq. You have to marry first. Americans will want me to do this [sex] first and I won't. This is why I want to go back to my country and get married there and then maybe come back.

School

This is how my grandpa remembers school here in Wisconsin:

> He quit in sixth grade
> to get his life in gear
> and learn a trade.
> Grandma went to high school
> but her family made her leave,
> to work and not be a fool,
> wasting time on what she wouldn't need.
> I am glad these days
> are in the past.

The Dawoods all began school when they were 6 years old. Mahira liked the 4-hour sessions:

We had Friday off because for the Muslims that is holy. But on Sunday we wouldn't go to school because we go to church. We don't have summer vacation, but we got 15 days off at the end of the year. There were six grades but we didn't call them that. You got a card every year saying if you pass.

Sarjon went to school the longest:

I went to primary school for 6 years and then secondary for 4 and then 1 year of tech. In primary school, we had a small English lesson, learned the alphabet and names of different things. Every year we got more stuff to learn, but I only knew a couple words until I came here. They [the school] wanted you to know everything around you, they tell you about what happened hundreds of years ago, teach you physical science, geography, math, I remember these.

Boys and girls were in classes together, but the importance of school for each gender differed greatly. Few girls made it past the elementary grades, because it was seen as more important for them to learn from their mothers how to raise a family. Many boys also quit to support the family or learn a trade.

Imagine coming and finding that the language of instruction has changed. This is what awaited Mahir when he started school in 1995:

> I was always in the same school with Mahira. But, when it changed to Kurdish I tried to go to a different school because there were more Christians there. At that school, you can speak Kurdish in class, but if you speak Assyrian, the teacher won't say anything. Some teachers were Christian. Mahira was going to quit. I hated school more because it was all Kurdish. I could speak it but couldn't read and write it as good because it all used to be Arabic.

Upon their arrival to the United States, Sarjon kept stressing one word as the key to their success: education. For him, Dunya, and Munir, this meant English as a Second Language (ESL) night class at Fox Valley Technical College.

Dunya still attends ESL two nights a week and is pleased with her success: "Teacher tells me I learn fast. I learned this in 2 days (pointing to her name in cursive), cursive is easy for me. [In Iraq] the teachers are really mean. They hit you and it was always Arabic. I didn't like it."

Sarjon quit ESL, unsatisfied with the teaching, but would like to further his education in the future: "I really like to learn. I like to learn computers, too, but I know it's very hard. I don't know anything about it, I don't know how to use it, so far. Someday when my English is better I can think of what else I can do. Maybe I can go to college too, or start my own small business."

While Sarjon dreams of school, the high-school students in the family want to get rid of this nightmare. Samir, Mahir, and Hushniya began at North High School, and Mahira followed them there this year from Tippler middle school. They have all asked Sarjon's permission to quit. At 19 years old, Samir is legally old enough to quit. Samir has exercised this right by skipping school for a week while Sarjon was in California and by calling in sick occasionally: "I tell them, no, you have to go. They want to work but I tell them go to school and you will get a better job. Don't worry about working now."

They understand what is expected of them, but reject the standards and reasoning that they hear all around them. It may be a case of teenage rebellion but they have their own ideas of what is best for them. Caught between their desires and the school's has led to an even standoff with neither side advancing. They are told they are doing great, but still are in the same low-level ESL class where they started.

Mahira is the only one that is not in the lowest ESL level. She started North High School in the intermediate level, but doesn't feel successful:

> I know what school is like now. I understand a lot but people still look at me differ-
> ent. I think some people don't talk to me because I'm in ESL and they think that
> they are better or something. I get As and Bs but it doesn't matter because ESL
> means I don't speak English good. I tell them [teachers] I just want to try regular
> classes. They say that I will get lost and not understand. Maybe, but to go to college
> and be smart you can't be in ESL. This is my third year. I can't stay in ESL my whole
> life. Once I leave [school], it's not ESL. I want it to be like this now, like real life.

Mahir has given up on school and doesn't think a diploma is even important. His brothers did fine in Iraq and are supporting them without diplomas
here, too: "In Iraq you can quit whenever you want, no one tells you to go
or says you need a diploma. And I didn't have to go in the morning like here.
I could pick, so I went at ten."

When Mahir wanted to switch schools in 1995, he took responsibility and
asked the other school if he could be admitted. He wants to choose what he
has to do here, too.

Mahira also remembers feeling free after school: "We play in the street
with friends, stay up late and just go outside with them and play games. You
can walk everywhere, my friends and family were really close by."

Our country's fixation with the automobile and devotion to building
around this convenience restricts the Dawoods from getting where they want
to go. Mahir loves the YMCA. It is only 10 minutes away from his home, by
car, not by foot. Mahira's best friend lives in Neenah. This is a short distance
by car, but for two 14-year-olds, it is like waiting for a commuter flight that is
always delayed. They understand that there is nothing they can do about this
until they get their driver's licenses and a car.

> They still dream in Assyrian, wishing they would wake up there.
> Here their past efforts are erased
> starting over in a strange place,
> where reading and writing English are judges of the race,
> while their hearts, inner thoughts, and dreams remain,
> scaling their childhood peaks a world away.

New Home

Sarjon misses some family, but remembers struggling to get by in Iraq. He recalls that supermarkets were bare and goods and foods were very expensive:

There if you have money everyone likes you, they want to be your cousin. If you don't have anything, nobody wants you. You are hungry, many times at night we sleep and we don't have anything to eat. We don't have no money to buy food. My uncle, aunt, I ask them if they need help (so we can work), but they don't do anything. So that's why I don't want to go back there. I don't think we will ever go back, I'll spend all my life here. Maybe I just go back for visits. I'll always come back here.

When they left Iraq Mahir was 14 and Mahira was 12. They were looking at their lives in terms of friendships. Some days kids were cruel, but their was always someone to play with to erase this pain. Now, they are 17 and 15, and their attitudes and comments are influenced by what they are going through in school. They feel safer here, but want the best memories from both countries.

Mahir disagrees that people are better here:

Kurdish people are nice, they are nice, everybody people. My friends were both Kurdish and Assyrian in Iraq. We go everywhere. Play soccer together, walk together, go everywhere together. Here everyone is with one girl, that's all. I got a couple friends but they don't do a lot with me or talk to me a lot. I don't know why. Sometimes I say "Hi" at school but they just keep walking, maybe they don't see me. I don't know why.

Yet, they have good days here when these feelings are forgotten. Both of their favorite memories here are of experiences they never could have had in Iraq. Mahira loved going to a friend's birthday party sleep over at a hotel in Appleton. They went swimming in the hotel and shopping at the Fox River Mall. Mahir enjoyed sports camp at the university last summer. They played basketball, tennis, and went swimming. Mahir's season on North High School's soccer team, and Mahira's choir concerts are the highlights of their school experiences.

Sarjon is tired, but smiling as he thinks of his job: "I do work a lot but I like my job. Now I am kind of like a boss. I get to tell a couple of people what to do."

Mahira is grateful for their new home and accessories that they never had in Iraq, like cable TV, a computer, and three cars. But, she thinks that they have paid more than money for these: "We used to play everything together—me, Samir, Mahir, and Hushniya—but now they all work. At night everyone is too tired and we have to get up so early. We don't sing or play games as much. There aren't as many fun parties here."

> When my dad went on the road
> to drive semi-truckloads,
> I missed him so much,

He used to be there
to play catch with
and watch my basketball games.
Then he was gone every day,
making money miles from home.

Mahira remembers never feeling alone.
Now, she wants me to stay all day
so she is not alone.
Work has taken her brothers and sister away,
and neighbors her age never give her a second glance.

Conclusion

Sarjon was faced with a dilemma. He keeps stressing that education is the way to future success, but the reality is that Lark needs a babysitter when he gets home from Head Start at noon. Munir had been providing this service while he worked nights at the YMCA, but his new job was too good to pass up.

In Iraq, Hushniya was already providing this service. Sarjon sees women working in many different jobs here, and realizes that there are opportunities for girls here too. Yet, he still believes that it is more important for Samir and Mahir to become educated, but did not expect Mahira or Hushniya to be obligated to stay home.

Sarjon thought the solution came to him one day:

Samir came again and says he quit school. I say, no, you have to go, you have to go. He says no. So, I tell him "fine you can quit and watch Lark." He say "No, I go to school." Hushniya hears us and said she'd watch Lark and go to school at night with Dunya. She said she could just go back next year, when Lark is in school all day. But, I don't want her to have to quit. I know she likes to learn, everyone does. Maybe even Samir. Day care would cost us a lot of money but I don't want her to quit.

Hushniya is pleased with this arrangement, however: "I'm so happy. I watch Lark and his friend and Sarjon and his friend's mom both pay me. I also work 40–45 hours at McDonald's. I'll be rich. When me and Samir get our licenses, Sarjon will help us buy a car and then we'll share."

By her teachers' accounts, Hushniya was an enthusiastic student. Her final report card was mainly all As and Bs. These are above average grades but they were not up to her standards: "My English still is bad. I'm still in the same class, so I'm not doing good."

Hushniya worked hard and did all of her assignments, so she feels that she just can't master school. Her teachers miss her and probably wish Samir was gone instead because he and Mahir still maintain that they don't care to be in school. They are running from the fear that Hushniya is facing: that maybe their best isn't good enough.

But the Dawoods are survivors. They vent their anger, and cry tears of sadness. Yet their confidence and moments of happiness keep them optimistic. Listening to them has taught me that life is a matter of perspective; it's how you look at what is coming at you.

> How we judge others
> is up to each of us.
> I believe the secret to doing right
> is in Sarjon's insight:
> Respect all people
> And they should respect you, too.

Postscript

Mahira, Lark, and I were sitting at McDonald's enjoying ice cream cones. Mahira was upset because at school she feels very left out in her mainstream classes. "Everyone looks at me and talks to me different, just because my culture is different. It's like all that matters." Suddenly, "the light bulb went on," just like my fellow members of the dominant culture everyday I interpret the world based on my experience and make value judgments on what I see. That these thoughts and actions are rooted deeply in the cultural norms I have lived under my whole life was an obvious reality I had been oblivious to for so long. I began to think of all of the people who I never talked to or got to know, just because of labels I subconsciously put on them. I thought about how much more fun we may have had together compared to the people I chose just because they seemed more "normal" to me.

It was through seeing myself as a cultural storyteller that the Dawoods and I began to understand each other. We finally saw the important things, that we are good people who enjoy each others' company and can grow together. Each of us has a story shaped partly by our own choices and framed by the cultural setting we were cast in. Interpreting the Dawoods' story was done best through sharing with them my story reflective of the dominant culture. Sarjon would compare the views and explain the functionality of their practices. As a future social studies teacher, my revelation that the dominant culture is an "invisible hand" that often distorts understanding, is a message that through documentation of ethnographic research I can share with all students. Reflecting back to my multicultural class in college, I remember two of my classmates complaining that the whole university is "too into culture" and that learning about differences divides the nation. Culture is inescapable; we all are subjected to it, and react in tune to it. When this reality is not shared among students, the result is Mahira's feelings of isolation.

Until being introduced to this project, the term *therapy* conjured up pictures of dim rooms with long couches and the deceitful looking doctor trying to help patients understand their messed-up minds. Therapy was something I did not want any part of, that was certain. Not that I don't fit the criteria of having a messed-up mind, but I do not feel up to the idea of understanding things that are painful and scary. The revelation of the atrocities that the Dawoods were subjected to in Iraq, and the United States's broken promises to the Kurdish people led to feelings of guilt on my part. Sarjon arrived here with reservations about trusting Americans. Addressing the stress involved in discussing this issue was necessary for us to move forward in our relationship. This experience has provided me with hope and consolation, and I learned the need for teachers to embody the role of a cultural therapist who seeks to help understand difficult issues and leads the way toward making this new understanding a positive factor in life.

Just as this project has influenced the way I view myself as a teacher and person, it has also impacted how I see myself as a Caucasian American. In the past, it was easy to fall into the mindset that the way I think, eat, and live are "right" and must be upheld. Overcoming food, customs, and beliefs that were foreign to me led me past these fears. What I found in the Dawoods is what I see in myself; that we are all people living with ties to our past, engaged in the present, and developing a vision for the future. It is this common bond that I feel the need to address as teacher. Although the details of the past and present are as unique as each individual, the vision that students form can include a place for everyone. It is as a border crosser that I believe the teacher can help bridge together a vision among students that values diverse histories and understandings.

In the 2 years since our project ended, the Dawoods and I have had some good times playing games, watching TV, and going roller blading. Sarjon is still working at the same job where he has since gotten a raise and promotion. Dunya was maintaining fulltime employment at Silver Creek Meat and is expecting a baby girl, whom they plan to name Lara. Samir did not return for his senior year of high school. He has moved out of the family's home and is living with friends and working two jobs. Hushniya has begun to work full time at Silver Creek Meat and part time at McDonald's. Due to her busy schedule, she has not pursued further education. She is planning to marry Dunya's brother in Greece in April, 2000, and then file papers to bring him to the United States. Mahir and Mahira are continuing their high-school education. Mahir is set to graduate in May, 2001, and Mahira in May, 2002. Since meeting the Dawoods over 2 years ago, our friendship has grown. I leave this project with a new vision and new friends.

REFUGEES FROM KURDISTAN:
SUGGESTED READINGS AND WEB SITES

Amnesty International. (1995). *Iraq: Human rights abuses in Iraqi Kurdistan since 1991*. New York: Author.

Brogan, P. (1989). *World conflicts*. London: Bloomsbury.

Chailand, G. (Ed.). (1993). *People without a country: The Kurds and Kurdistan*. New York: Olive Branch Press.

Cockburn, A., & Cockburn, P. (1999). *Out of the ashes: The resurrection of Saddam Hussein*. New York: HarperCollins.

Gunter, M. (1992). *The Kurds of Iraq: Tragedy and hope*. New York: St. Martin's Press.

Gunter, M. (1999). *The Kurdish predicament in Iraq: A political analysis*. New York: St. Martin's Press.

Human Rights Watch/Middle East. (1995). *Iraq's crime of genocide: The Anfal Campaign against the Kurds*. New Haven, CT: Yale University Press.

Jentleson, B. (1994). *With friends like these: Reagan, Bush, and Saddam, 1982–1990*. New York: Norton.

Kashi, E. (1994). *When the borders bleed: The struggle of the Kurds*. New York: Pantheon Books.

Kelly, M. (1994). *Martyrs' day: Chronicle of a small war*. New York: Vintage Books.

Kreyenbroek, P., & Allison, C. (Eds.). (1996). *Kurdish culture and identity*. London: Zed Books.

Laizer, S. (1996). *Martyrs, traitors and patriots: Kurdistan after the Gulf War*. London: Zed Books.

McDowall, D. (1996). *A modern history of the Kurds*. London: I.B. Tauris.

Meiselas, S. (1997). *Kurdistan: In the shadow of history*. New York: Random House.

Simons, G. (1994). *Iraq: From Sumer to Saddam*. New York: St. Martin's Press.

Thornhill, T. (1997). *Sweet tea with cardamon: A journey through Iraqi Kurdistan*. London: Pandora.

Timmerman, K. (1992). *The death lobby: How the west armed Iraq*. London: Fourth Estate.

Kurdish and Assyrian Web Sites

Clark, R. (2000). Report to UN Security Council, re: Iraq (January 26). http://www.iacenter.org/rc12600.htm

Contains information on the formation and activities of the Assyrian American National Federation. Catalysts for the migration of the Assyrian people are also discussed. *This site is maintained by the Assyrian American National Federation headquartered in Chicago, Illinois.* www.atour.com/aanf/docs/history.htm

Information about Kurdish language, history, culture, music, and liberation movements. *Maintained by Kurdish Information Network (KIN)*. http://www.xs4all.nl/~tank/kurdish/htdocs

Link to information on the regional issues influencing Kurds. Also, features links to a variety of information. http://www.kurdish.com

Looks at the Catholic diocese in Iraq as well as their historical roots. http://www.knight.org/advent/cathen/15745c.htm

News article highlighting cases of Kurdish attacks on Assyrians in Northern Iraq. *This information was provided by the Assyrian International News Agency.* www.aina.org/cases.htm

Provides geographic, historical, and political information on Kurdistan. Seeks to foster Kurdish-American friendship and understanding. *Official site of the American Kurdish Information Network (AKIN).* http://www.kurdistan.org

Seeks to foster Assyrian awareness by looking at International Human Rights Violations Against Assyrians in the Middle East. Also, contains historical, political, cultural, and linguistic information on the Assyrian people. *This site received the Britannica Internet Guide Award and information is compiled by the Ninevah online staff including links to Britannica and articles published by the Irish Times.* www.nineveh.com

A Kosovar Family

REFUGEES FROM THE BALKANS

Some of the most documented atrocities of the 1990s have taken place in the states of the former Yugoslavia. Perhaps the light skin of the combatants and the proximity to western Europe have caused the tragedies in the Balkans to receive more international attention than the slaughter and starvation of millions in parts of Africa. Nevertheless, the Balkans wars hold the ignominious distinction of introducing the concept of *ethnic cleansing* to the world's attention. The practice behind this euphemism has been full-scale genocide, massive destruction of villages and towns, and the displacement of hundreds of thousands of refugees.

The Balkan mountains are home to a number of ethnic groups, including Serbs, Slovenes, Croats, Bosnians, and Albanians. These groups speak a variety of languages and dialects, and have religious practices ranging from Catholicism among the Croats, Orthodox Christianity among the Serbs, and Islam among the Bosnians and Albanians. The region has historically been a battleground between competing empires and world views, and events in the 1990s were marked by the memories of the bloody struggles of the past.

On June 28, 1389, Christian Serbs were defeated by Muslim Turks at the Battle of Kosovo. This defeat would result in hundreds of years of foreign domination for the Serbs, and they would find ways to commemorate the date in years to come: As part of a long struggle to regain and maintain independence from the Austro–Hungarian Empire, the Archduke of Austria was assassinated in Serbia on June 28, 1914. On June 28, 1989, in an event that would help lead to the break up of Yugoslavia, Slobodan Milosevic spoke before an estimated 1 million Serbs in Kosovo, telling them that "Nobody, either now or in the future, has the right to beat you" (Campbell, 1999, p. 152; see also Rogel, 1998).

Kosovo and its Neighbors

The Serbian policy of ethnic cleansing used in the 1990s had its precursors earlier in the century. During World War II, in the German-allied puppet state of Croatia, 500,000 Serbs were exterminated in concentration camps. German forces in Yugoslavia organized Albanian and Bosnian Muslim units; some Serbs joined the fascists and others, the resistance. The wars and policies of the 1990s "have their roots in this World War II period of political, ethnic, and religious brutality" (Rogel, 1998, p. 12).

Josep Broz Tito, a popular resistance leader, came to rule a nonaligned communist Yugoslavia from the 1940s until his death in 1980. Tito managed to keep a nation of diverse ethnicities together in a federation of six republics—Serbia, Croatia, Slovenia, Montenegro, Macedonia, and Bosnia–Herzegovina—and two autonomous units within Serbia, Kosovo and Vojvodina. In the 1980s, however, Yugoslavia found itself in economic and political turmoil with no one of Tito's popularity or stature ready to take control.

Ethnic nationalism filled this power vacuum. Elections in 1990 brought nationalists to power in Serbia, Slovenia, and Croatia. Bosnia–Herzegovina was divided among Muslim, Serb, and Croat political factions. In 1991, Croatia and Slovenia declared independence, and 4 years of warfare and ethnic cleansing followed, with the ethnically diverse land of Bosnia–Herzegovina bearing the brunt of the conflict, just as it had during World War II. The United Nations response to events in the Balkans was late, limited, and generally ineffectual. The United Nations declared "safe havens" in towns, such as Srebenica, then stood helplessly by as Serb forces came to round up the men and boys (many were found later in mass graves) and rape the women. However, the Dayton Accords, signed in 1995, brought at least a shadow of peace to the countryside.

The issue of Kosovo, however, remained to be settled. The population of this region is 90% Kosovar, or Albanian Muslim, yet when Milosevic removed the state's autonomy and declared martial law in 1989, political and military power reverted firmly into the hands of the Serbs. By 1998, the Serbs were using the supposed threat posed by the Kosovar Liberation Army (KLA) to justify the razing of villages and displacement of the Kosovar population. This process was accelerated dramatically in the spring of 1999 when, under the threat of armed intervention from NATO, the Serbs began ethnic cleansing in earnest, and over 1 million Kosovars fled the region. A NATO bombing campaign, which targeted Serbian Yugoslavia, succeeded in removing Serbian military and police presence from Kosovo, and hundreds of thousands of refugees were able to return to their homeland to rebuild the destroyed villages they had vacated a few months before. As the Serbian forces retreated, the KLA military materialized, and soon Serbian refugees were clogging the roads, fearing reprisals.

Jessica Wade-Martinez has worked with an extended family of Kosovar refugees at their restaurant for the last few years. In the following chapter, she focuses on the lives of the Sutaj family, and the events that led to their flight from Kosovo.

FIG. 6.1. The American Table Restaurant, Oshkosh, Wisconsin.

FIG. 6.2. Jessica Wade-Martinez.

— THE SUTAJ FAMILY —

Jessica Wade-Martinez
With the Sutaj Family

When I first began working at the American Table, I didn't realize what an impact it would have on my life. This was just a job for me at first—a way to support myself while attending college and away from home. I knew that my bosses were from a different country, but I was working there for a few months before I even found out where. It wasn't until I began thinking about this dialogic teacher research study that I actually discovered where my boss was from and what a difficult life he and his family had lived before they came to Wisconsin. We became very close and would spend many hours talking about our dreams, our hopes for our own lives and for others, how we want to change the world, and what we want to leave behind when we die.

Through all this, I became close to this family, including their extended family. I participated in birthday parties and homecomings. I was there when the restaurant opened and other joyous occasions. I was there through the tears, fears of death, and the strangeness of depression. This family became my surrogate family while all of us were away from home.

The head of the family was Zahn. He is a very intelligent and pensive person. He is an activist for the Albanian people in Wisconsin. He grew up in Macedonia and attended college in the United States. Prior to bringing his family to the United States, Zahn was an independent filmmaker in his home country, Yugoslavia. He had to leave his country because he often filmed conditions under the oppressive government and the damage it did to his people. Even after Zahn moved his family to the United States, he went back to Yugoslavia to film more atrocities. He told me about a time when he got caught trying to bring his tapes out of Kosova and into the United States:

> I was sitting next to a guy I knew. I traveled with him often. He was a businessman. And we were waiting on the plane to take off, you know? When we saw police cars, I know why they are there. I said to my friend, "You see, they come for me." (*Zahn laughs.*)

> My friend says, "No, they don't come for you." He didn't believe me, but I knew. So we were waiting there on the plane, we were delayed because of the police. On the plane comes this big fat police man huffing. (*Zahn laughs again, puffing up his cheeks and teetering back and forth to imitate the fat police officer.*)

I said to my friend, "Just watch. He comes to get me." The police comes right up to me still huffing because he was running. He says "Open your bag"—looking for contraband. I had a small bag with me which had my zoom lenses and things for the cameras. So I open the bag and show him the lenses and I told him what they were. He said, "Where's the film?" So he took me off the plane where they had my suitcases. They searched through and found my movies. They said, "Oh what's this?" and I told them that I had been filming my family. You know, I had a birthday party. I *did* have a birthday party on the film … along with a lot of other stuff (*Zahn laughs*). I really had to talk my way out of it and convince him it was just my family on the tapes. They kept my film anyway and let me get back on the plane.

They must have seen the lenses in the x-ray. And they know me … I've taken film out before. They know to watch for me.

History

The area known as Kosovo has been seen as a source of strength and survival by both the Serbian and the Albanian people. Both groups of people have occupied Kosovo for hundreds of years. In the 20th century, Albanian population figures in Kosovo have ranged from 70 to 90%. (Jacques, 1995) Kosovo is an area that has two languages and two religions. The Serbs speak Serbo–Croatian, use the Cyrillic alphabet, and the religion is Eastern Orthodox. The Albanians speak the Albanian language, use the Roman alphabet, and the religion is Islam.

In 1389, after the Battle of Kosovo with the Turkish empire, the Serbs were forced to move out of Kosovo if they wanted to hold on to their Christian religion. The Albanians, who shared the Turks' Muslim faith, were allowed to take control of Kosovo and it's surrounding area, which was called Albania. The Turks divided Albania into four provinces: Shkodra, Kosovo, Manastir, and Janinë (Frosina information network 1996).

In 1878, Russia defeated Turkey, putting an end to the Ottoman Empire. The Treaty of Berlin split up Albania, which had been part of the Ottoman Empire. What was once all of Albania now formed Montenegro, Serbia, and Macedonia (all under Serbian rule). Bosnia and Herzegovina became part of Austria. The leftover parts remained Albania (Frosina information network, 1998).

During the Balkan Wars, which began in 1912, Turkey finally lost its remaining European territory, including Macedonia and Albania. Albania became an independent country, while Serbia, Greece, and Bulgaria fought over the remaining Macedonia. Greece gained the southern part of Macedonia (Janinë). Serbia gained Kosovo and northern and central Macedonia (Balkan Wars, 2000). After this division of lands, life for the Albanians living in

Kosovo became difficult. No longer were Albanians allowed to use their own language or have any written works in their own language.

With the advent of the Federal People's Republic of Yugoslavia under Tito, a new constitution was developed dividing Yugoslavia into six republics. Because of this reformation, Albanians were recognized as a "distinct national group." The Albanian language was also recognized as one of the official languages of Kosovo, as a language equal to Serbo–Croatian. Albanian schools were also opened. At this point in time, illiteracy rates in Kosovo were up to 90%. Kosovo was seen as having "social backwardness" (Prifti, 1999).

Albanians had only 2 years of freedom from persecution; in 1948, Tito's vice president, Aleksandar Rankovic, began to encourage the hatred toward the Albanians and Croats in Yugoslavia. He believed them to be "politically disloyal and 'potentially subversive'" (Prifti, 1999, p. 74). Albanians were tortured and imprisoned once again. After the fall of Rankovic in 1966, Albanians in Kosovo were again granted rights as Yugoslav citizens. They were allowed to use their language again. They were even allowed to study in their mother tongue at the University of Prishtinë (in the capital city of Kosovo). But they were not allowed to become their own republic. Anyone openly supporting a "Republic of Kosovo" was imprisoned for 15 years or more (Prifti, 1999).

In the 1990s, policies of *ethnic cleansing* were directed against Albanians living in Kosovo by the Yugoslav government of Slobodan Milosovich. Ethnic cleansing is defined by Mark S. Ellis of the Central and East European Law Initiative (CEELI) and the Coalition for International Justice (CIJ) as "a policy of using any type of force or intimidation to remove these targeted persons from a given area, and then to inhibit them, from returning … ethnic cleansing can involve … the intent to destroy a group in whole or in part" (Atrocities and the Humanitarian Crisis in Kosovo, 1999).

Prifti (1999) showed accounts of Albanian men being tortured while the Serbian police screamed, "never again will you have Albanian children!" It was even forbidden to give an Albanian child a name connected with Albanian history. Walls surrounding Albanian homes were bulldozed by Serbs because the architecture was said to be a restraint to "interethnic solidarity" (Prifti, 1999).

By 1997, 70% of the Albanians living in Prishtinë were unemployed. By October, 1998, two third of all villages in Kosovo were either seriously damaged or completely destroyed (Prifti, 1999).

Schooling for the Albanian Child, Teacher, and Parent

I met Sulë, his wife Havë, their twin daughters, Arta and Arjeta, and their sons, Visar and Valon, through Zahn. Sulë, the former director of waterworks in Pristina and outlying areas, and Havë, a former teacher, were working 12-

to 16-hour-days cleaning office buildings in Oshkosh and nearby. Arta, Arjeta and Valon were working at the American Table restaurant, and Visar was attending the high school and working part time. My quotes were taken over time while working with the family at the American Table restaurant, while teaching English lessons to Arta, and while interviewing the family formally in their small apartment. When I talked to Havë and her husband, Sulë, Sulë's sister, Hedije, translated.

In 1990, the Serbian Parliament shut down approximately half of the schools in Kosovo to Albanian children. In 1991, 396 full-class primary schools, 454 four-year and annex primary schools, 56 secondary schools, and 7 teacher training and engineering schools were closed. The University of Prishtina was also closed down. In August, 1991, 6,000 Albanian teachers were laid off (Ramaj, 1997). One afternoon, after our English lesson, Arta and other family members shared these thoughts about schooling in Kosovo:

> Arta: We didn't have schools. We had to study in people's homes. We had to sneak there. A man had a big house and [would] give his house so that the Albanians go to school. I started school in a house when I was 15 years old. I study 6 years. I was out for 1 year because I was sick. They thought I might have a tumor because I was so sick. But it was because of our school. We had to sit on the cold floor in the basement. No heat, no windows. There were no books, no nothing. If a Serb police see you with books or school papers, they [would] beat you.

Arta's mother Havë worked in the public schools as a teacher and a school psychologist. She taught sociology, Marxism, philosophy, psychology and logics. She taught only to Albanian students, whereas Serb teachers taught only to Serbian students. The school was segregated.

> Visar: They split the (elementary) school—put a wall in the middle of the school. One side Albanian and one side Serbian. Now the wall is broke. The kids started fighting. They beat me so hard.
>
> Havë: The kids would wake up at 6:00 in the morning to go scared to these houses [the schools]. They were so stressed and the kids lost interest. How you gonna go to school if you don't have a book or a desk? [They have]—nothing. But … (*Havë and her husband Sulë smiled at each other, remembering a proud moment*).
>
> Sulë: About 2 years ago, we saved $100. It was the most exciting moment! We were able to buy Visar a table—a work table so that he didn't have to sit on the floor. A desk to write on because he was a very good student.
>
> Havë: We have our own stores, schools, and media, separate from the Serbs. They came and took it over. I found work at one of the

schools that remained open. But how was I supposed to teach while from the windows, we could see little villages burn down? And the kids would look so sad ....

Every day, my students came bleeding ... bleeding because they got beat up by the Serb police while they were coming to school. Even my co-workers would come to school like that. [The Serbian police] said, "Because I can." Serbian people would get in a group and beat up our kids coming out of school. The Serbian police, because we didn't have our own police, instead of breaking it up, they would help to beat the kids up. As a parent and a teacher, first as a parent, we felt very desperate. We could give our kids nothing—except maybe a little word or a hug or one moment. And when my kids needed me the most, I could give them nothing.

As teachers, we were supposed to be the role models. My kids talked about their teachers all the time. We were trying to be the role models—but even that stopped after a while because we were at home, desperate. We went to work just a couple of days. We lost hope from our personal lives and from the teachers and co-workers. We couldn't give them no more hope. But we tried ... we tried.

Every day I had an average of five or six kids come into my classroom with a bloody hand or face. I could do nothing for them—I didn't have a first aid kit. Every day an average of five or six kids would not come to school. They couldn't come because the police were there or their family went into hiding. Ten years of living, as my kids went to [the school], wondering, "Are my sons and daughters going to come home alive?"

Sulë: Students going to private houses, no books, no texts, and parents with no jobs. No prospect for anything. And the kids, the kids, oh! They lost so much. When we were in school, we had to work with the Serbs. But for the younger generation, they had enough. It was 1990 when the worst came. Parents had no job, no nothing—no heat, no phone, and no electricity. The water went on and off. We would take [water] from the lakes. No hospital. Everything became expensive.

Havë: Everything changed in our life. People and kids started to change. They took us out of our jobs by force. We used to have our own gazette and TV station. That closed too. They closed all Albanian media. So, this way, we would be isolated. We didn't know what was going on in our own country. Our family was close, like 1 hour driving. I wouldn't see my family in 1 or 2 months because we couldn't go. They wouldn't let us. Sulë saw his mom twice in 3 years—it's only an hour drive! Albanian phones were out. I heard my Serb neighbor talking on the phone. He had everything [that] we didn't.

There are Serbs who have now left Kosovo and are now able to live easy for 50 years because they took money from Albanians. They knew that the Albanians would pay any amount of money to survive.

Sulë: [Albanian] families would share money. People who were rich would supply friends and family with food and money. Farmers would send food free to us. The schools were supported by people, no government money. When they could, people who had some money would help the kids out with supplies, like buy them chalk. Havë taught without a paycheck. Sometimes she made $100 from someone who had money, but that would be the only pay she would see for 3 to 4 months. People lost hope. Parents couldn't offer [their children] nothing. Nothing! I heard of so many adults and young adults who [commit] suicide these past 10 years. They hang themselves—going crazy.

The beginning of the end was Drenitza. It was the fighting there in 1998. It got worse when people started telling other [countries] what was going on in Kosovo.

Fear

In the United States, I was working at the American Table restaurant. I remember 1998, when the whole atmosphere of the restaurant changed. Zahn became depressed and would not speak for hours. Sometimes, he would talk about what was going on over in Kosovo, but none of us really understood. Often he would sit for hours, staring into space, not hearing or seeing anything that was going on around him. He would spend days on the phone, calling the White House. He even got me to call the White House on occasion. He installed TVs in the restaurant and would spend hours watching CNN updates.

About this time, Hedijë called her brother, Sulë, in Kosovo and told him to take the kids out [of the country]:

I said, "Please, take the girls!" because I had heard of girls getting raped. But the girls didn't want to leave. They wanted to leave all together [as a family]. They thought, "This whole thing—it's going to stop. They can't take us out of our own home, our own land. This cannot happen."

We told them to go to Zahn's family house in Macedonia. Zahn told them, "You can stay at our house. We have a big house. Just leave!" They said, "No, it's just around the villages. They won't come here because, then, the world will know. That's not going to happen. It won't go so far. Not another Bosnia will happen."

Later, in the safety of their small apartment in Oshkosh, Havë, Sulë, and their children would describe the fear and humiliation of those days.

Havë: Maybe you have a Serb neighbor and you drink coffee with them. But everything changed in a day. Serbian neighbors were now putting Albanians on trains and buses, taking us out of the country. And the Serb neighbors were clapping.

Visar: Humiliation.

Arta: When people left a house in Kosovo, they were put on trains to Macedonia. No food. Babies died. When I see all of the people, [they were] freezing and asking for help. How could I help? They wanted me to take their babies.
My father went to a restaurant near my house. A Serb man had his best friend. [My father] saw all the blood. The friend said, "Sulë, help me!" My father wanted to help him, but the man put a gun in his mouth and said, "Go home if you want to live." My dad went and got the son of the friend and my brother and some other friends and went out looking. They couldn't find him.
Just ask my father about this friend [now] and he cries. He says, "I'm never going to forget—he said, 'Sulë, please help me!', and I didn't help him."

Havë: When the bombardment started, we were so happy. But when the bombs stopped, the Serbs would come into our houses.

Visar: When NATO started bombing, I was laughing. But then, when you were sleeping, here come the Serbs in the night with masks. I was playing soccer outside when the alarms started. I thought, "It's nothing. They will never come here because then Europe and the United States will know what they are doing." I thought "They will be scared of that." But then, I saw the tanks coming. When night came, I kept a knife in my hand. I was only 14 then. I'm 16 now.

Arta: Before that, I was crying about all of the people in Bosnia when I read about it in the newspaper and see the news. But we didn't know what is war. They say that by the time they get to us, the Serbs already ate their dinner—that Prishtina is the dessert.
It's different when you see. When you've been to that place. When you have been all the time in war. When we listened at night. When we heard NATO. When they stopped ... oh, the Serbs! We waited at the window. We waited for death. I lived 1

week waiting for my death. Then I thought, Why am I waiting for death? I have to live! Why to be dead? I didn't know what to do.

Sulë: When the bombardment started, we all started getting ready. We slept in our clothes. We [were] looking out windows, just waiting for that moment. We didn't know if they were going to take us or … we didn't know what was going to happen.

We took pills—antidepressant pills because we were all going nuts. I would say every night to my family, "Just hold on to yourself. Don't lose your mind." But, I [didn't] think none of us would survive. I told my kids, "If they kill me and Havë, you guys escape—don't stay there."

Arta: I would stay awake all night thinking, "Who is going to come and kill us?" I remember seeing people … it's hard to leave your house. All of my beautiful and ugly days were in that house. I had with me a big knife. I thought, "If anybody comes in my house, I just gonna kill myself. I don't want to wait and see what happens. If someone were to try and hurt my brother, I'd kill myself." I stayed awake and wait[ed].

My uncle lived five minutes away. I couldn't go see how he was, we didn't have a phone. We were in the same place but I didn't know if they were dead or alive until I made it to Macedonia [where] I called Hedije in America and another aunt in Switzerland. My grandmother and aunt and uncle hid out in a cabin in the woods. My aunt and uncle carried [my grandmother] on their backs.

Havë: Our town looked so dead. The houses, no one could move. Just police cars. They would play their music high. Serb nationalism music was so loud. The words in their music said, 'We gonna come and kill you' and other … bad things.

We hear that they were taking people out of their houses close to us and killing them. So we said, we are going to leave. We heard they were taking out pretty much everybody.

I had neighbors upstairs. He was a Serb. The night before [we left], I went upstairs and asked, "Do you know what will happen? Please, can you save us?" He said, "Me, help you? What are you waiting for? You should [have left] before! I can guarantee you nothing …"

Leaving Home

Sulë: We left our home early morning—the first day of April, 1999. That morning we left. Some [people] walking, some [people] in cars. All together with police guiding them and watching them. We left our home with about $100 in our pockets and just the clothes on our backs.

Arta: We left at 6 o'clock in the morning. One of [my older brother] Valon's friends came to my house crying. His mother was sick with breast cancer. I said, "Why are you crying?" He said, "The police came to my house and told me that we had to leave or we will all be massacred."

Oh ... I cried. I knew his mother was too sick. He and his mother left. I saw my father ... scared because he remembered how Dijë told him to take us kids [from the country]. When the war started, he said, "What have I done to my kids? Why [did] I do this to my kids?"

Visar: The police had come to our neighborhood and told [us], "If you don't leave, we are going to kill you." My dad said, "Come on, let's go."

On our drive [to Macedonia], we saw all of the houses burning. I didn't care about that. I only thought about myself. I thought I would be dead. The Serb police stopped us. We thought they were going to take the car—it was good—Italian. We thought we would have to walk. But they knew my father because 10 years ago, they worked for my father. They said, "Let them go."

Havë: That night, the line stopped because Macedonia didn't want to take us. But, still the police wouldn't let us stay there. We had to wait 3 days. We could not sleep. They would come, take people out of their car, separating man from woman and say, "Give me everything you have. Jewelry, money, whatever, because if you don't, I will kill your child."

Arta: One woman was with her family. Serbs came and told them that they had to pay $100 per person to live. They only had $300. The two daughters said, "[keep] the boy—so that we have a man to carry on the [family] name." The Serbs only let the mom, the dad, and the boy off the train in Macedonia. The woman walks around the camp, asking, "Where are my daughters?"

They took us away from our cars. People couldn't enter with cars. We began to walk. They separate the women from the men. Everyone started walking. When we got to the border, my mom said, "We are just going to drop you kids in the border and then me and Sulë will go back home." We kids said, "No, if you go back, we go together." How am I going to live my life knowing my parents are dead? No way. I'm not going to do that.

Havë: I felt so bad. Why I leave my home and my country? I feel like I can't do anything for my country. I'm not a person ... I can't stick with my country. That night was so scary. We didn't know if we would be killed. If we didn't have each other—brother, sister, family—we wouldn't be alive. When I saw all the people there at the border, I saw Auschwitz.

Arta: It was hard hearing all of the kids crying all night. I remember Visar. I don't care about myself, but Visar—he ask for food.

Visar: I was eating just cookies. I have no food. Just cookies. I ate cookies for 2 days. A lot of families have nothing to drink or eat ... I feel so sorry ... They didn't have milk, the babies. The babies just drink water. They didn't have nothing else.

Arta: "Something for the kids!" [parents] were screaming and crying. We saw houses and wanted to see if they had any food. But nobody was there. The house was messy because Serbs had been there. Some people came in and took [what they could find]. For me, it was nothing to eat for 3 days.

They didn't let us into Macedonia. Lines and lines of cars waited. They let only a few people in each day.

Sulë: I went with everyone to the border but then I went back to the car because it was not my car. I borrowed it from a friend. The police almost kill me because I went back for the car. Police almost kill me. I ran away.

Arta: I walked to Macedonia and saw all Albanian people. All these Albanian people, no clean place, no [clean] clothes, the camps. I cried and said, "They left their houses and they came here—just to be alive. Thank God I am alive."

No Man's Land

When they got to the camp, an Albanian family from Macedonia took some refugees to a school where the Sutaj family waited to find out what happened to their father and their aunt whom they had not seen since they went back for the car. Every day, they went back to the camp to search.

In the United States, all of us at the restaurant waited nervously. We saw all of the people freezing in the camps on the news. We saw the families looking for lost relatives. My heart broke when I heard a little girl on TV crying because she couldn't find her daddy. I think that this week of waiting, watching the camps on the news hit Dije the hardest out of all of the family members waiting at the American Table. She had received a phone call from her nieces saying that they didn't know where her brother or mother were. Local news reporters came to interview her. She worried that her aging mother had died along the walk and that her body would never be found. She told reporters, "If she is out their dying somewhere ... If she had died before, I could cry at her grave. Now, they could have thrown her some-where and I don't know where she is."

Reunited at the American Table, Arta and Dije talked about searching for relatives in the aftermath of ethnic cleansing.

Arta: When I went back to the camp, I saw people I knew. They told me they saw my father. It was easier for me because I knew my father was alive. I had never seen my father cry. I heard he had been crying. I didn't want to see [him crying].

I didn't know if my grandmother was alive. Where is my family? I saw a friend in the camp and we cried. He said, "Hey, Arta! Can you imagine this? Yesterday we were at our own place. Today we are here at this camp." Now, you see we are separated and spread out all over the world.

My aunt was let out of the camp because she is a woman. My sister and Valon went to the camp to find my father and aunt. They stopped at a restaurant for some water and my aunt was there. They didn't recognize her because she was in the camp in the rain.

My father was in the camp, in the rain, for 8 days. He just could-n't go because there was Macedonian police, the same as Serbian police. A big tank went to the camp to bring the people water. One of the men who brings the water, my dad said [to him], "Please, can you help me? My family is waiting for me."

Dije: Albanian people from Macedonia were bringing people water and bread in the camp and were beaten by Serbs for helping the Albanian [refugees]. Sulë escaped in a truck that was filled with water ... he and some friends got into the tank. The man just took him some place and opened the tank. He said, "Now you are safe."

Sulë went to every house and school and church where the Alba-nian refugees were staying, looking for his family. Somehow, they got together and got to Zahn's house. They called me that first night there. That's when I found out. I was so happy, I cried when I heard his voice. But, his voice sounded so gravely because he had not slept. And he had this TB test and tested positive. He was on medication for months.

I felt so helpless. Where could I send money? I couldn't do any-thing and my family's dying! I felt like a nobody. They finally made it to the United States.

Havë's brother with three kids and a wife hid out in a basement and stayed in Kosovo the whole time. We didn't know for 2 months if they were alive or dead. They are OK.

People hid in the mountains. The Serbian government didn't allow humanitarian aid to go and bring food. The first French truck went in with food after 3 months. How these people survived, I don't know.

This man Zahn made a movie about—he's [in the U. S.] now—lived in a cave for a month and a half taking just water and flour and putting it in the sun, making like a pita. He saw some kids … kids found him. But he was so weak, he couldn't do anything. He was safe. NATO was already there.

Now it's better for [my nieces and nephews]. When they first came here, I couldn't talk to them sometimes—they would yell and scream. Their self esteem was so low. They couldn't do anything.

Return

I asked Havë if she goes back to Kosovo, will she return to teaching.

Have: Yes. My students will be able to come to school. There will be no problems. Everything is going to be OK. It's going to take time to forget these past 10 years. I hope the next years will be good for the teenagers.

Arta: All this I say to you, I will say to my children. I'm never going to forget Kosovo. It hurts too much in my heart. Now I know what happened in Bosnia. I am not American. I know I am Albanian. Sometimes I don't like to remember these ugly 10 years, but I'd like [my children] to know. I want my children to know what kind of life we have as Albanians.

I met one lady in the school [we stayed in after crossing the Macedonian border] who told me about her village in Kosovo. She told me about how the police came and took her husband. He yelled, "Please, help me!" And they killed him.

THE ARKAN OF THE WASHITA

Today I am shadowing Visar Sutaj as he attends classes at the high school. Presently he sits beside me in the cafeteria during his second-period study hall. He is about 6 feet tall, slim, with short, trim hair, and brown, serious eyes. He wearing a dark blue sweatshirt with "American Yachting" and the sketch of a yacht in white, tan corduroy pants, and black and white all-purpose tennis shoes. When we begin to chat about his upcoming test in American history, the study hall monitor comes over and asks us to move to the periphery of the room; we are breaking the silence imposed on the other 60 to 70 students gathered there that morning.

His test is about "the Old West." Visar shows me the study sheets where the names of 10 important figures of that era are graphically organized, along with spaces to fill in their dates of birth, death, nicknames, and importance. Who are these ten figures? Somehow I am not surprised to find the usual suspects: Buffalo Bill Cody, Wyatt Earp, Billy the Kid, Calamity Jane, George Armstrong Custer. They are all White, and, save for the gunslinging Calamity Jane, all male. In the small rectangular space corresponding to Custer's "importance," Visar has written, "Good at surrounding Indian villages."

I shared with Visar that I had been to the site of one of the villages that Custer had surrounded: Black Kettle's camp on the Washita in western Oklahoma. On Memorial Day, 1999, we met Sam and his family when we stopped at the "Battle of the Washita" historical marker. Sam is descended from the few southern Cheyennes who survived Custer's predawn raid. The camp was home mostly to women, children, and elders. Black Kettle, a peace chief, kept an American flag and a white flag flying before the entrance to his tipi, but these protected neither him nor his defenseless people that morning. Custer's troopers surrounded the village and then rode in to attack, burning lodges and shooting at anyone who tried to escape through the snow-covered landscape. Brown (1970) described how Custer followed his orders to "kill or hang all warriors":

> In a matter of minutes Custer's troopers destroyed Black Kettle's village ... To kill or hang all the warriors meant separating them from old men, women and children. This work was too slow and dangerous for the cavalrymen; they found it much more efficient and safe to kill indiscriminately. They killed 103 Cheyennes, but only 11 were warriors. They captured 53 women and children. (p. 164)

When the news of this "victory" reached the East, Custer was known as the "hero of the Washita." "Custer," I suggested to Visar, "was the Arkan of the Old West."

Visar's eyes harden in recognition of the name of one of the most wanted Serbian war criminals. "You know," he said, "We believe that Arkan is not dead." He said that many Kosovar refugees feel that Arkan's so-called assassination was faked to allow him to avoid prosecution for crimes against humanity. Rogel (1998) described Arkan in this way:

> The war in Yugoslavia was made to order for those like Arkan. Thugs, criminals and those used to operating lawlessly thrived in the chaotic environment ... If Arkan was not the initiator of the war's ethnic cleansing policies, as some claim, he and the Tigers were responsible for some of its most bloody atrocities. (p. 107)

Visar tells me, "Arkan was responsible for the deaths of 300,000 people. Do you know, when Arkan's soldiers stopped me and my dad and held us for questioning, they did drugs right in front of us?"

"They say that many of Custer's soldiers were drunk on whiskey that morning on the Washita," I respond. "Maybe, to do the things they are being asked to do against defenseless people, some soldiers have to be drunk or on drugs."

Dialogues that reconsider our histories and our present from multiple perspectives are fundamental to what Freire (1998) called

> a universal human ethic in teaching, an ethic not afraid to condemn the exploitation of labor and the manipulation that makes a rumor into truth and truth into a mere rumor. To condemn the fabrication of illusions, in which the unprepared become hopelessly trapped and the weak and defenseless are destroyed ... an ethic affronted by racial, sexual, and class discrimination. For the sake of this ethic, which is inseparable from educative practice, we should struggle, whether our work is with children, youth or adults. (pp. 23–24)

I shared with Visar that my 5 year-old son liked to play another story from the Old West with his action figures. Many days when I returned from work he would ask, "Dad, can you play 'The Day Custer Died' (the Battle of the Little Big Horn) with me? You be Custer and I'll be Crazy Horse." When next I see Visar at his aunt's restaurant, he smiles, looks at my family and asks, "Which is the son who likes to play history?"

THE AMERICAN TABLE

Cass, the slightly cynical but playful eldest member of the wait staff pours a cup of coffee with one hand, pours ice water from a pitcher in her other hand, and, noticing that I am writing, adds, "Betcha I can make that wet!"

I look up, smile, and respond, "I have no doubt of it." She laughs and walks off.

I sit in a small booth in the American Table restaurant, which lies on the northern edge of downtown Oshkosh, Wisconsin. Despite the dividing wall between the smoking and nonsmoking sections, there is a big, open feeling inside. There are windows on all sides, looking out on the Burger King, Main Street, and the vacant lot where Jessica's old apartment once stood. We were there the Saturday morning that they knocked the apartment building down. Orion, Ariana, Marcel, Kathleen, and I watched the show as bulldozers and wrecking balls did their work. Jessica, then our waitress, came over and shared her memories of the place, a short stop on her journeys.

Jessica has been gone from town for over a year now, and Saturday mornings are not quite the same without her at the restaurant. First, she was in Mexico, doing her student teaching on an island. Now she is working near Green Bay, and waiting for her Mexican fiancé to be allowed to cross the border for a visit. Others, too, have left the American Table: Lyana, the tall, attractive woman from Kosovo whom Jessica referred to as her sister, was one of the first of the Kosovars to return to Pristina. I remember her when she first started working as a waitress, and we were impressed with the speed at which she picked up the nuances of the local English dialect. She laughed when we complimented her on this, saying that she hoped to teach English back in Kosovo. Arta and Arjeta, the Sutaj twins, have also returned to Kosovo with their family. They were always sweet to our children, telling us that "Ariana is an Albanian name," and insisting on walking around the restaurant, holding baby Marcel. Even Raul, the friendly Mexican busboy who seemed to practically live in the restaurant, is gone. Zahn told me that Raul had gotten in a fight at a bar, and had not come back to work. I remember all the times Raul would play with Marcel on the floor, and the time he came over to our house for an English class, and we talked about going for a long bike ride some day when he could get off from work. It is hard for me to imagine him fighting anyone, and I wonder if he is still in town, or on this side of the border.

Despite the departure of people we have known—and it leaves a hole in our lives—the American Table still is a refuge for us. It is a place where children are loved, street people are welcomed, and conversations in different languages can be heard. There is a feeling of community here, a sense of possibility. As metaphor, *the American table* represents the promise of a world where brothers and sisters, distant cousins in one human family, of different colors, cultures and languages, can eat together, work together, and build a new society together. At the dawn of a new millennium, we can dream of the day when the last real borders that exist are crossed, the borders that separate our minds and our hearts.

Martin Luther King Day, 2001

REFUGEES FROM THE BALKANS:
SUGGESTED READINGS AND WEB SITES

Anzulovic, B. (1999). *Heavenly Serbia: From myth to genocide*. New York: New York University Press.

Bennett, C. (1995). *Yugoslavia's bloody collapse: Causes, course, and consequences*. New York: New York University Press.

Bringa, T. (1995). *Being Muslim the Bosnian way*. Princeton, NJ: Princeton University Press.

Campbell, G. (1999). *The Road to Kosovo: A Balkan diary*. Boulder, CO: Westview Press.

Cohen, L. (1997). *Broken bonds: The disintegration of Yugoslavia and Balkan politics in transition*. Boulder, CO: Westview Press.

Demick, B. (1996). *Logavina Street: Life and death in a Sarajevo neighborhood*. Kansas City, MO: Andrews & McMeel.

Emmert, T. (1990). *Serbian Golgotha: Kosovo, 1389*. New York: Columbia University Press.

Filipovic, Z. (1994). *Zlata's diary: A child's life in Sarajevo*. New York: Viking.

Gutman, R. (1993). *A witness to genocide*. New York: Macmillan.

Honig, J., & Both, N. (1996). *Srebrenica: A record of a war crime*. New York: Penguin.

Hukanovic, R. (1996). *The tenth circle of hell: A memoir of life in the death camps of Bosnia*. New York: Basic Books.

Human Rights Watch. (1997). *Bosnia and Herzegovina: The unindicted: Reaping the rewards of ethnic cleansing*. New York: HRW Publications.

Kaplan, R. (1993). *Balkan ghosts: A journey through history*. New York: Vintage.

Rieff, D. (1995). *Slaughterhouse: Bosnia and the failure of the West*. New York: Simon & Schuster.

Rogel, C. (1998). *The breakup of Yugoslavia and the war in Bosnia*. Westport, CT: Greenwood Press.

Silber, L., & Little, A. (1997). *Yugoslavia: Death of a nation*. New York: Penguin.

Stiglmayer, A. (Ed.). (1994). *Mass rape: The war against women in Bosnia–Herzegovina*. Lincoln: University of Nebraska Press.

Vickers, M. (1995). *The Albanians: A modern history*. New York: Tauris Press.

West, R. (1941). *Black lamb and grey falcon*. New York: Viking Press.

Web Sites: The Balkans

Albania and the Albanians. The Frosina information network, May, 1996. http://www.frosina.org/infobits/advmay96.shtml

Albanian history. Albanian.com. 1998. http://www.albanian.com/main/history/index.html

Albanian language education in Kosova: Letter sent from Abdyl Ramaj, Secretary of the Commission for Education of Democratic League of Kosova, and Head of Parliamentary Commissionfor Education, Science, Culture and Sports of Kosova to

Frederico Mayor, UNESCO General Director, as well as to several embassies in Belgrade. Alb-net.com. August 12, 1997. www.alb-net.com/freekosova/education/index.htm

Amnesty International (2000). New amnesty international report says NATO committed war crime during Kosovo conflict. http://www.amnesty-usa.org/group/balkans/ref8.html

"Balkan Wars." *Encyclopœdia Britannica*. 2000. http://www.britannica.com/bcom/eb/article/4/0,5716,12124+1+11972,00.html?query=balkan%2 wars also http://www.britannica.com/bcom/eb/article/8/0,5716,47188+1+46112,00.html?query=kossovo%20polje

A Frosina infobit: The battle of Kosova (1389). The Frosina information network. April, 1998. http://www.frosina.org/infobits/kosova13.shtm

Human Rights Watch (2000). Municipal Elections in Kosovo (October). http://wwww.hrw.org

Juka, Dr. S. S. *Kosova: The Albanians in Yugoslavia in light of historical documents*. 1984. http://www.alb-net.com/juka2.htm

KOSOVO BATTLE: Excerpts from different Encyclopediae. Srpska Mreza. 1996–2000. http://www.srpska-mreza.com/

STUDENTS INDEPENDENT UNION OF THE UNIVERSITY OF PRISHTINA. Bujar Dugolli, President of the Students Independent Union of the University of Prishtina. Sept. 22, 1997. http://www.informatik.tu-muenchen.de/~januzaj/uni-prishtina/monitor_e.html

III
Extending the Dialogue

7

Extending the Dialogue: Pathways for Change

The goals of our dialogic teacher research project are to facilitate an increased understanding between mostly European-American teachers and the diverse immigrant and refugee families they serve. This understanding comes at both a very personal level as well as through a critical awareness of ways in which economic, political, social and cultural relationships within and across groups and nations affect the lives of newcomer families and all members of society. This chapter synthesizes aspects of cultural storytelling, healing, and border crossing, as raised in the four family narratives; it suggests implications, or pathways, for change, for teachers and teacher educators, immigrant and refugee families, and communities, schools, policymakers, and society. If we seek to build a society where all are welcome, broader, inclusive dialogues are needed to promote understanding and social justice in schools and communities.

CULTURAL STORYTELLING

The four family narratives in this volume demonstrate the teachers' roles as cultural storytellers, sharing their own autobiographies as well as collecting and interpreting the stories of students, families, and communities. The authors of these texts collected stories using ethnographic techniques, arranged texts as stories, and used forms, ranging from prose, to poetry, to representation as dialogue, to present stories in a powerful fashion. Perhaps most importantly, the voices of family participants are fundamental to these texts, highlighting the narrative dialogue taking place.

As they represent and interpret family narratives, the authors of these texts use their own autobiographies to further dialogue with family members, as tools of self-reflection, and as a critical challenge to readers. Four of the authors—Faye Van Damme, Katie Hinz, Judy Mehn, and Jessica Wade-Martinez—grew up in Wisconsin, and they discuss how the places and the people in their lives have shaped their cultural understandings. Maya Song-Goede has lived most of her life in the United States, but her own refugee status and acculturation provide her with additional insight into the border-crossing experiences of another.

Faye Van Damme starts her narrative with the telling contrasts of January 15, 1983, between her birthday party in rural Wisconsin and Chan Lor's escape across the Mekong River in Laos. Ironically, both scenes are characterized by innocence: Chan Lor sees suffering, death, and destruction of families, neighbors, and villages as the Hmong are pursued by the Laotian army. Yet we still see him as an innocent boy caught up in the aftermath of a failed, American-backed war effort. Faye Van Damme is engaged in the most innocent of pursuits, a childhood birthday party with friends and family. At the time she is also innocent, as are her parents and most Americans, of the events taking place in Laos, of the genocidal war conducted against the Hmong, of their squalid life in the camps in Thailand, and of the reasons why these people, who will so often receive the epithets of "gook" and "chink," and be told to "go back to China," are here in the United States, the home of their erstwhile ally in war. Van Damme's willingness to underscore her own innocence of events serves as an effective prelude to a cultural dialogue, which both informs and transforms her thoughts and practice as a teacher.

Throughout her narrative, Katie Hinz seeks to compare and contrast her life, beliefs, and values with those of the Dawoods. She has lived her entire life in the same house on the south side of town, whereas the Dawoods have moved from place to place, driven by the search for employment, security, and freedom from persecution. She contrasts the flat Oshkosh and the brown waters of the Fox River with the mountains of Zakho and the clarity of the Tigris. She writes of the similarities of her own Catholic faith with that of the Dawoods, though theirs has been made the stronger by persecution. In her empathetic reaction to the loneliness felt by her friend Mahira in America, Hinz shares her memories of her father's absence:

> When my dad went on the road
> to drive semi-truckloads,
> I missed him so much,
> He used to be there
> to play catch with
> and watch my basketball games.
> Then he was gone every day,
> making money miles from home.

Her sharing of personal stories and experiences with the Dawoods over time has led to the creation of a dialogue that is critically conscious, yet suffused with friendship.

Judy Mehn effectively contrasts the lip service paid to cultural diversity and understanding with the actual practices of people she grew up with in Madison, Wisconsin, a city known for its progressive attitudes. She writes of fear: "So many people, at least in my family, just don't want to get to know another culture. Anything different from them they are afraid of (although they would never admit they are afraid)."

Mehn channels this reflection concerning her own upbringing into the dialogue, and thus extends empathy to Angela Gonzales' concerns about the lack of tolerance for Spanish speakers, Mexicans, and nonmainstream cultures in Wisconsin.

Maya Song-Goede draws on her own experience as a refugee to help understand the life of a Mexican immigrant. She has experienced firsthand the shock of relocation to another country where one's linguistic and cultural norms are turned upside down. As a Hmong American, she has experienced racism, ethnocentricity, and linguistic intolerance. In addition, she has a special insight and interest in immigration laws and practices, which enables her to engage with Angela Gonzales and Judy Mehn in a dialogue that opens a window onto fundamental questions of immigration rights.

Who are our immigration laws designed to allow in? To keep out? Why do we extend (albeit grudgingly) refugee status to Hmong, Kosovar, and Kurdish peoples fleeing political persecution in their countries, yet we have systematically denied refugee status to persons fleeing regimes friendly to the United States? There are Mexican people—in Chiapas and elsewhere—who have reason to fear political persecution from the government and the army, yet they will not be granted refugee status. The hundreds of thousands of El Salvadorans and Guatemalans who fled persecution by U.S.-backed governments in the 1980s weren't considered political refugees, either. Rather, they joined a flood of brown-skinned people who inhabit an illegal netherworld within the American economic juggernaut and democracy, denied rights to living wages and decent housing and healthcare, denied the rights of citizenship, constantly in fear of being deported and thus, they are compliant on the job and relatively invisible in the community.

Stories shared in the family narratives provide an ethnographic portrait of cultural histories, cultural adaptations, and cultural changes underway. Clearly these stories provide meaning for a variety of audiences: They help the teller to reflect on and better understand the events they are living through; they educate teachers, as collectors of stories, about individuals and cultural groups; and they serve as guideposts for the generation of refugee and immigrant children growing up in an American culture that stresses the paradoxical values of individuality and conformity.

Sharing stories with interested listeners allows refugees and immigrants to confront traumatic experiences in the past as well as to put their own current struggles and experiences in America in perspective. The stories of refugee escapes from war-torn countries are vivid, horrifying, and immensely tragic, yet their telling seems to be necessary as part of a recovery process. For Chan Lor, the memories of hunger, fear, and survival in the jungles of Laos have been tempered by time as well as a return to his native land for a visit. The Dawoods' stories of their departure from Kurdistan cannot be separated from the feelings they have for the loss of their mother's life; yet, they are also able to remember with nostalgia the parties, dances, and weddings in Iraq. For the Sutaj family, the tragedy and horrors of their escape from Kosovo are real and immediate in time and feeling, and occupy much of the dialogue they shared with Jessica Wade. Yet, the nature of their refugee situation is such that they have been afforded the possibility to return their homeland, filled with its tragedy but renewed in its hopes. For Angela Gonzales, Mexico does not conjure up such images of war and flight, but rather the beauty of family relationships, the land, and the widespread poverty that makes everyday life a struggle to survive. For all of these families, life in the United States, though far from perfect, offers a time of respite from previous struggles. Their dialogues with teachers offered them a time for sharing, reflection, and reconsideration of the past.

Teachers on this project learned a good deal about the world from which refugees and immigrants come. Beyond the general geographical and cultural details that are part of the narratives, nuances are also present that allow critical perspectives: We learn, for example, that, when captured by the Mekong River, Chan Lor and the Hmong people with him were placed in a village, given homes and lands to farm, and children were sent to school—all part of the new communist order in the country. The Hmong who came to the United States were mostly fleeing communism, it is true. Yet, there is undeniable evidence that the communist regime provided important services for those people with whom it was not actively at war.

The Dawoods stories take us to Iraq, the "rogue nation" of choice for the United States in the 1990s. Sarjon was tortured by soldiers of the Baathist regime, and his father was killed fighting in the war against Iran. Yet, Saddam Hussein's government responded to the father's death by giving the family money to build a house. Assyrians, such as the Dawoods, were allowed freedom of religious expression and given important posts in the government. Until their implication with the Americans and other elements of the occupation force in northern Iraq, the Dawoods could be said to have gotten on well with a government that the United States has sought to demonize. The economic hardships Sarjon reports—the lack of food-stuffs in the stores, for example—reflect the early results of the U.S.-led economic sanctions against Iraq. In his report to the U.N. Security Council, Ramsey Clark attributed the destruction of Iraq's water, electrical and other systems and 10 years of sanctions with the deaths of 1.5 million people. On the widespread malnutrition in Iraq, Clark (2000) wrote:

> The sanctions target to kill or injure infants, children, the elderly, and the chronically ill ... Food distribution from a comprehensive rationing system controlling staples delivers 1,100 calories per day for every person throughout the country, Kurd, Sunni and Shi'ite Muslim, Christian, Jew, rich, poor, alien, with special rations for infants, pregnant women, the severely malnourished, and others with special needs. The poor cannot significantly supplement their food rations. In 1989, daily caloric intake in Iraq averaged 3,400. (p. 4)

As to the destruction of the Iraqi people, which the U.S.-led war and sanctions have accomplished, Clark (2000) asked, "If this is not genocide, what is?" (p. 4).

The economic hardships that cause millions of Mexicans to immigrate to the United States provide a background to the poignant story of Rosa Gonzales Ramirez. With her husband, she leaves her children behind to work as an undocumented alien in the United States. When enough money is saved, they send it to a *coyote*, who would provide the false documentation for the children to enter the country, asleep, so the border patrol wouldn't check their documentation carefully. They move to Oshkosh to be close to Angela's family, but the "good life in America" continues to elude them.

Rosa first crossed the border in 1992, a significant year for people throughout the hemisphere. It marked 500 years since the arrival of Europeans, and led to official celebrations and widespread organization of continued resistance to economic and political oppression. The year was doubly significant for Mexicans, for in 1992 the federal constitution was amended to legalize the sale of *ejidos*—communal plots that were established after the Mexican Revolution. In order to open up Mexican lands for corporate investment, these *ejidos* could now be sold to the highest bidder. With the NAFTA agreement, tariffs on U.S. agricultural imports have been lifted, and heavily subsidized U.S. corn now floods Mexico's markets. Ten million Mexican farmers could be displaced from the land by the year 2004, and, significantly, the number of Mexicans living in extreme poverty rose from 14 million in 1988 to 22 million in 1997 (Willson, 2000). Evidently, the economic oppression of Mexican people by Euro-American outsiders continues after 500 years.

Yet the destruction of Mexico's traditional agricultural system, upon which 70% of Mexican farmers rely, is only part of the story. Under the guise of a war on drugs, U.S. military equipment is used to foster the military occupation of large areas of Mexico's rural south, especially in Chiapas. Mexican soldiers receive special counter insurgency training at the infamous School of the Americas in Georgia, and use these skills to conduct *low intensity warfare* against Zapatista base communities. What is low intensity warfare? Soldiers invade rural villages, order everyone out into the surrounding jungle, and then burn houses, poison wells and destroy crops. Then they leave. Suspected insurgents are raped, tortured, and killed (Willson, 2000). Does it surprise anyone that millions of Mexicans would choose to leave rural communities that have been economically devastated, and sometimes militarized, as a condition for Mexico's entry into free trade with the United States?

For the Sutaj family, stories of persecution, survival, and escape from Kosovo have an immediacy that is not lost on the reader. Through their stories, we can put faces on the tragic tale of millions of displaced people in the Balkans, on the thousands who have died, and on the villages and cities destroyed as part of the policy of ethnic cleansing. To know that the Sutaj's story has now taken them back to Kosovo is heartening; yet the task of rebuilding a divided society will be daunting. NATO's intervention in Kosovo first exacerbated the flow of refugees, then eventually made it possible for Albanian Kosovar's to return home. Yet, NATO must take responsibility for its own record of war crimes in the bombing of Yugoslavian civilian targets, and its mixed record as an occupation force on the ground in Kosovo, if ethnic tensions are to be eased (Amnesty International, 2000; Human Rights Watch, 2000). Furthermore, the United States must reevaluate its use of depleted uranium, used in missiles fired during this war and the war against Iraq. Several NATO soldiers have died of leukemia since their exposure to depleted uranium, which lies scattered about the villages, streets and fields of Kosovo, a dangerous health risk to children and adults trying to rebuild their lives (Simons, 2001).

It is clear that these four families' stories have meanings they wish to share with their children. These stories compare material conditions of the past with those of the present: Chan Lor recounts his experiences, alone in the Thai refugee camp, looking longingly as parents bought their children trifles he could not have. Yet, Chan has persevered and now owns his own business, and perhaps this tale can be meaningful for socioeconomically disadvantaged Hmong youth, who see everyday the excesses of American consumerism displayed by their better-off classmates. Similarly,

Angela can illustrate the economic hardships of growing up in Mexico with the relative plenty enjoyed by her own children in the United States. For the Dawoods, the possibility of working hard, buying a house and some cars, and the feeling of being secure in their new home is a welcome relief. Yet, the long working hours in pursuit of this "good life" have taken their toll: Angela works at night, and cannot be at home with her children, and she worries about what is going to happen to them; Mahira laments for the times when her brothers and sisters could be together as a family, without being exhausted from working all the time: "We used to play everything together, me, Samir, Mahir, and Hushniya, but now they all work. At night everyone is too tired and we have to get up so early. We don't sing or play games as much. There aren't as many fun parties here."

Perhaps, in the sharing of their stories, these refugees and immigrant families are seeking ways to provide a bridge for their children growing up in America, a bridge between American individualism, consumerism, and English and the family-centered culture, language, and values of their homelands. Chan Lor says:

> Deep inside me I still know who I really am and where I came from. As a parent, I help preserve my culture by speaking Hmong at home to my kids, telling stories of Hmong heroes and folk tales, keeping Hmong tapestries and embroideries, and practicing Hmong ceremonies like the Basi and shaman ceremonies.

Stories keep alive a memory of a people, and the practices of a culture, in a time when there is great pressure on all children and youth to conform to a world of Pokémon, Nike, and Nasdaq.

CULTURAL HEALING

Refugees and immigrants often enter the United States experiencing the posttraumatic stress of having faced warfare and the struggle to survive in their homelands. Once here, their lives continue to be marked by economic, linguistic, and cultural conflict. To survive, they must work long hours, often at low-paying, dangerous jobs, and the costs of food, housing, and fuel constantly undermine any prospects they may have of saving money. They are surrounded by a world of English, at the workplace, in school, in shops, and in the media. The use of their own languages is publicly discouraged, sometimes by law. Many school officials go further by telling parents to quit using their language at home, as it will hold back their children's education. The majority of immigrants and refugees are also marked by their physical features, accent, and mannerisms as being different from the mainstream culture. For this, they endure open and covert racism and ethnocentrism at work, at school, in the street, and at home, watching the ways their particular group is misrepresented, or nonexistent, in the media.

Refugee and immigrant communities are places where the process of healing begins. We learn that extended family relationships are important in the newcomers' home countries and instrumental in their adjustment to life in the United States. We learn of Chan Lor's relatives who help him escape from Laos, and support him as a young boy without parents in the United States. Similarly, Angela Gonzales speaks of the role of her sister in helping her get started in California, and Angela's own role in supporting and advising Rosa when she moves with her family to Wisconsin. Dije and Zahn were instrumental in both bringing the Sutaj family to Oshkosh as well as helping them find work and housing once here. The Dawoods fled Iraq after the deaths of their father and mother. Coming to Oshkosh without other family to support them, they do their best to support each other as brothers, sisters, and guides.

Of all the narratives in this volume, the Kosovar refugee experience is the most recent, and the Sutaj family has the most immediate need to deal with the stress of having survived a war experience that was humiliating, life-threatening, and tragic. Significantly, the entire family seems eager to share their remembrances of their last days in Kosovo:

Havë: Maybe you have a Serb neighbor and you drink coffee with them. But everything changed in a day. Serbian neighbors were now putting Albanians on trains and buses, taking us out of the country. And the Serb neighbors were clapping.

Visar: Humiliation.

Arta: When people left a house in Kosovo, they were put on trains to Macedonia. No food. Babies died. When I see all of the people, [they were] freezing and asking for help. How could I help?

Jessica Wade-Martinez allows them space to pour forth their stories of this tragedy with little interruption, serving as an active listener to this stage of the cultural healing process. Significantly, she and the Sutaj family have a strong relationship founded on working together and friendship, and this contributes to the open dialogue established.

The Dawoods are also in recovery from an ordeal that cost them their parents, their friends, and their homeland. Sarjon is the victim of torture. All family members remember the feeling of being persecuted for their religious beliefs, and having their home language forbidden in schools. Yet, through their dialogue with Katie Hinz, one can feel their resiliency; they are, as Hinz points out, survivors, and they want to do well in their new home. The challenges they now face are adjusting to school, new social mores and gender roles, and making time for their family amid the false urgency of American economic life.

Significantly, all of the Dawoods attending high school have asked their eldest brother to give them permission to quit. After learning Assyrian in the home, and having intermittent schooling in Kurdish and Arabic, the Dawoods are faced with learning English, their fourth language, while learning challenging academic content at the high school. All save Mahira are in the lowest ESL level classes. Mahira writes about the frustration of understanding school but feeling trapped:

> I know what school is like now. I understand a lot but people still look at me different. I think some people don't talk to me because I'm in ESL and they think that they are better or something. I get As and Bs but it doesn't matter because ESL means I don't speak English good. I tell them (teachers) I just want to try regular classes. They say that I will get lost and not understand. Maybe, but to go to college and be smart you can't be in ESL. This is my third year. I can't stay in ESL my whole life. Once I leave (school), it's not ESL. I want it to be like this now, like real life.

Katie Hinz's interactions with the Dawood family began as she volunteered as a tutor with the family members at the high school. Trained to be a social studies teacher, she knows firsthand the academic challenges they face. She offers support and suggestions to help them manage the schooling process, but she also offers the healing power of friendship and shared experiences. Woven throughout their dialogues together are places where, in the discussion of school, boyfriends, or family time, Hinz and the Dawoods share ideas and a healing relationship of words and activities together. There is a healing power in their dance together on the hilltop, on the first day of Spring. Hinz writes:

> I tried to dance and follow the human chain's
> fluid rhythm circling around and around,
> but I was tapping when they were hopping.
> I wished I could fade into the ground,
> but their support kept me from stopping.

Mexican immigrants such as Angela Gonzales often face discrimination based on their physical features, their culture, and their language. Much of this is due to the proximity of Mexico to the United States and the perceived threat, reinforced by many politicians and the mass media, that Mexicans and the Spanish language represent a threat to our way of life. Angela shares her frustration over the treatment she receives from Anglos on the job, both in restaurants and in factories:

[When] most people noticed that I didn't speak good English they started making fun of us, or asking, "Where you from," or "Do you have papers?" "Are you legal or not?" ... If you don't speak English right, forget it. You're lost. But one thing that I noticed ... If I work by myself I am okay. Even the White people [are] close, and they talk to me, and they want to make me feel like I am at home. But I notice that when there are two or more Mexicans, they try to keep away. For example, if we are speaking in Spanish ... the White people go, "What are you saying?" And I say, "I don't know. We were just talking." And they say, "Did you say something about me?"

Maya Song-Goede and Judy Mehn listen as she speaks, and they ask questions to encourage her to discuss openly the discrimination she has faced. Moreover, the researchers attempt to provide ideas for Angela in terms of what to do when faced with discriminatory practices in housing and on the job. Perhaps as importantly, these researchers provide the therapy of laughter: "Rosa ... says she was waiting for her life to get better, and she hasn't seen it yet. Someone mentions, 'the good life' in America, and we all laugh."

Significantly, both Maya Song-Goede and Judy Mehn are able to step outside the dominant culture and see both the difficulties and the humor posed by this search for the American dream, as popularly conceived.

Chan Lor has had the most time to reflect on his story of exile and renewed life in the United States. Sharing this story with Faye Van Damme, though, helps to continue the cultural healing process. Through all of these shared narratives, families realize that their experiences do matter, that they need not be invisible in American society, and that they make contributions to our society that others recognize. Chan speaks eloquently about the need of all Americans to embrace the variety of cultures in this country. He offers a vision of what we can become: "I see all the different cultures that are in the United States. It makes it a little difficult to understand why people hate one another when we are all human beings. We should be able to live together under one roof, but that is not the case because we (people in general) only like our own kind."

Refugees and immigrants such as Chan Lor have the potential to lead our society through the process of cultural healing which we so desperately need.

CULTURAL BORDER CROSSERS

As *cultural border crossers*, participants in this dialogic research process entered into unfamiliar territory, in space, in relationships, and in the realm of ideas. Van Damme, Song-Goede, Mehn, Hinz, and Wade-Martinez entered the world of refugee and immigrant homes and lives. The Lors, Gonzaleses, Dawoods, and Sutajes crossed linguistic and cultural borders to share their stories. Through dialogues and research, participants challenged the dominant meta narratives of our times with small stories and alternative perspectives on the lives of newcomers to America, their reasons for being here, and the U.S.'s role in the world.

The stories of refugees and immigrants challenge our perceptions of why people come to the United States. They did not all come to this country for handouts: The Lors, Dawoods and Sutajes were fleeing for their lives. Significantly, the United States had a direct role in causing the conflicts from which the Lors and Dawoods fled. Some, such as the Gonzales family, come here for economic reasons, yet they are often fleeing joblessness and poverty, brought on in part by their nation's increasing links to global capitalism. Many of the family members share their wishes to return to their native country some day, despite the traumas of the past. Chan Lor has returned to Laos for a visit; the Sutaj family has, it appears, returned to Kosovo for good.

These narratives also challenge our knowledge of cultural geography, and the various peoples who reside, and often conflict, within national boundaries. The Lors are Hmong, distinct from Laotians and one of several peoples residing in the mountains of Laos. Part of their recruitment by the CIA involved promises of more self-determination as a people. The Sutajes are Albanian, one of many ethnic groups with distinct languages and cultures inhabiting the former Yugoslavia. The particular history between the Albanians and the Serbs reflects the long-seated divisions, which still haunt the Balkans. The Dawoods are Assyrian Christians from Kurdistan, minorities among minorities. As such, they are alternatively persecuted by their Muslim Kurdish neighbors or the Arab Baathist regime ruling in Baghdad.

In addition, these narratives challenge teachers to rethink history and their place as educators in a contested world. We learn about the role of the Hmong in support of the U.S. secret war in Laos, the Hmong struggle to survive annihilation when their ally departed, and their journey to America. We learn about the role of the U.S. government and corporations in first building up Saddam Hussein's arsenal of destruction, and then using the invasion of Kuwait as an excuse to destroy the Iraqi people and nation. The Dawoods were fortunate to escape while they could, while there was still some food on the shelves in the early years of the economic sanctions that have led to so many deaths. We learn, in detail, of the horrors of *ethnic cleansing*, as practiced in Kosovo, while, for a time, the United States and much of the rest of the world watched. We learn of the long, troubled economic and political history shared between the United States and Mexico, wherein Mexico lost over half of its national territory in 1848, and where much of its lands, resources, industries and the lives of its people are in the hands of its powerful neighbor to the north.

Teachers need to know these contested histories. Without it, how can they hope to understand their immigrant and refugee students and families? With knowledge of these contested histories, teachers can become better educators of all youth and better liaisons to all families. They can help build a nation where we take seriously our responsibility for our own government and its actions. They can be leaders in imagining alternatives to global capitalism, which consumes human lives and destroys the earth, our only home, in the pursuit of profit.

PATHWAYS FOR SCHOOLS AND COMMUNITIES

In the past few years, various scholars have taken Freire's (1970) work in problem-posing education into ESL and bilingual education contexts (Moraes, 1996; Wink, 2000). In a special issue of the *TESOL Quarterly* devoted to critical approaches in the field, Pennycook (1999) suggested the need for "a pedagogy of engagement: an approach to TESOL that sees such issues as gender, race, class, sexuality, and postcolonialism as so fundamental to identity and language that they need to form the basis of curricular organization and pedagogy" (p. 340). Examples of such a pedagogy from the classroom include the development of problem-posing literacy practices with immigrant women (Frye, 1999), and acknowledging migrant students' lives in mathematics teaching (Trueba, 1998). Critical pedagogy also is woven into teacher preparation for those working with immigrant populations (Brutt-Griffler & Samimy, 1999).

Great challenges exist to those who would be border crossers, who would help students and families express and understand their own stories in the larger contexts of society. Educators are confronted by a world where the freedom to think, act, and teach critically is not often honored. In his foreword to Freire's (1998) *Pedagogy of Freedom*, Stanley Aronowitz asks, "What does freedom mean, especially in education?" (p. 18). When pedagogy means teaching to standardized tests, what is freedom? When school curricula is governed by the vagaries of the textbook industry, what is freedom? When young people and their teachers are forbidden from using their native language to understand the word and the world, what is freedom? In an era of globalized capitalist economies fueled by cheap, expendable workers, Freire (1998) wrote that we must make "a decisive NO to an ideology that humiliates and denies our humanity" (p. 27). He argues that teaching must be

> a profession that deals with people whose dreams and hopes are at times timid and at other times adventurous and whom I must respect all the more so because such dreams and hopes are being constantly bombarded by an ideology whose purpose is to destroy humanity's authentic dreams and utopias. (p. 127)

There are many ways to use extend the dialogues begun in this volume, to share the dreams and visions of newcomers with all Americans. Through critical dialogues about education and people's lives, the hopes and the authentic dreams of bilingual students and their families can be kept alive.

DIALOGUE JOURNALS

Journals offer a wonderful opportunity of engaging refugee and immigrant students in both literacy and a dialogic process. Dialogue journals are valuable tools for literacy development, which grows out of personal knowledge, diverse experiences, and interests, involves interaction with others, and takes time (Freire, 1970; Peyton & Staton, 1993; Vygotsky, 1978). These journals are also a source of information about students' cultures, activities and needs, as a private channel for honest communication, and as a means for resolving difficult classroom situations (Reed, 1993). With funds from a small grant, some colorful journals with blank pages were purchased and given to approximately 25 interested ESL and bilingual students in area districts. Over the course of the year, these students made regular entries in this dialogue journal exchange, which involves myself, a research assistant, and various students from my ESL and bilingual education courses at the university.

At the end of chapter 4 is a section from the dialogue journal of Beatriz, a student from Mexico, and John, a student at the university. Below is another excerpt from Ka, a friendly Hmong girl with black hair and eyes. One day I shadowed Ka from 7:30 a.m. until 3 p.m. at the high school. During five of her classes, she quietly filled in worksheets or quizzes. During one hour (U.S. history) she watched part of *Little Big Man*, a movie starring Dustin Hoffman. In her final hour, a business teacher attempted to engage students in active learning. While he worked out the kinks of the scenario up front, the majority of the class talked freely with each other, the first time this had occurred in Ka's classes all day. Of course, their topics of conversation had nothing to do with the exercise, and more to do with being a teenager. That day Ka wrote this in her journal:

November 9, 1999

Hello Dr.

Well I hope you felt better now cause we been sitting in class for pretty much the whole time. And thank you for coming I know it's not fun but thanks anyway.

Well today is kind of a headache day for me cause you know I don't really know what to do cause my first hour teacher wasn't here and the sub didn't really explain well enough so I could do the homework at home ...

Well I hope you enjoy the tour with me today and I'm sorry if thing doesn't go the way you planned. *Sib ntsib dua os* [See you later].

Bye,
Ka

Indeed, it was "kind of a headache day." It was the kind of lower track, meaningless educational experience that has been all too common in U.S. schools (Goodlad, 1984; Kozol, 1991; Oakes, 1995). Much of the current discourse about the education of bilingual students at the secondary level is driven by the need to, at best, to help such students succeed academically as they adapt to the mainstream. Yet, at what point do educators begin to question the dominant ideology that drives mainstream education as well as other social and political processes? For Freire, the neoliberal, capitalist ideology, so powerful at present in most of the world, limits the ways in which students can learn and teachers can teach: "From the standpoint of (neo liberal) ideology, only one road is open as far as educative practice is concerned: Adapt the student to what is inevitable, to what cannot be changed. In this view, what is essential is technical training, so that the student can adapt and, therefore, survive" (Freire, 1998, p. 27).

Rather, Freire (1998) urges the teaching of content in ways that bring forth the adventure of learning for teachers and students alike:

> The teaching of contents, undertaken critically, involves a teacher's total commitment to the legitimate attempt by the student to take in hand the responsibility of being a knowing subject ... a teacher committed to the adventure of bringing to birth in the student a person at ease who can articulate in his or her subjectivity. (Freire, 1998, p. 112)

Recently we tried to bring about six high school students, including Mahira, Visar, Ka, and Mai Lee, to a writing conference to talk about their dialogue journals, their lives, school, and their advice for teachers. Unfortunately, the session was canceled at the last minute, due to lack of interest on the part of teachers attending the conference. In order not to disappoint the students, Katie Hinz and I invited them to think about making a video. Ka and her friend Mai Lee came with Katie to my house, and began to brainstorm some possibilities. They imagined scenes from traditional Hmong villages in the mountains of Laos; life in the refugee camps of Thailand; their journeys to the United States, and their lives in Oshkosh. We hope to initiate this video project with high-school students this year.

DRAMATIC DIALOGUES

Drama has always been used to facilitate dialogue and to educate people. From the Hindu epics of the *Ramayana* (Narayan, 1987) to the exploits of Mexico's *Superbarrio* (Martinez & Gonzales, 2001), drama has been used to help audiences renegotiate the boundaries between themselves and their world. Drama has also achieved a strong place in language instruction, as it allows learners to step outside themselves and experiment with language as another character (Smith, 1984; Wessels, 1987).

One of the projects that was initiated during the dialogic teacher research was "Teaching NAFTA (North American Free Trade Agreement), Learning Students' Lives" from two sources: First, I have used improvisational theater before in an English as Foreign Language context in Ecuador. There, when students were asked to brainstorm plot lines for dramatization, the social, economic, and political situation of their country was always in the forefront. For example, they depicted scenes of public protest against U.S. interventionist policies, the corruption of politicians and generals, police brutality and torture. Yet, there was a comic genius alive in each scene, and students shared with me that much of their acting was inspired by Evaristo, an actor in the theater of the streets, who routinely made fun of those in power, especially the *gringos* (Hones, 1993). Secondly, I visited a bilingual social studies class at one of the high schools in our area. There the students, all recent arrivals from Mexico, were being quizzed on the material dealing with imports, exports, and international trade, as found in a rather dry economics textbook. The class was conducted in Spanish, the book was translated into Spanish, but I could see that the students were not making a connection. Yet, the lives of these students have been irrevocably marked by the vagaries of global economics.

"Teaching NAFTA, Learning Students' Lives" is a project meant to reconnect teachers and students to the economic, political, and historical contexts of their lives. It involves research into the historical, economic, and political relationship between the United States and Mexico, and the more recent repercussions of NAFTA felt on both sides of the border. It connects students with the curricula of social studies, language arts, math, and science. The project begins with a role play of the *Bully 4U! Awards*, which contrasts the behaviors that are typically rewarded in school with those rewarded in the global political economy; and culminates with a dramatic representation of the issues entitled *No me olvides, Amigo [Don't Forget Me, Friend]*. In this play, students are provided with the beginnings of a rough storyline they must fill out, scene-by-scene, working cooperatively and using their own life experiences and knowledge gathered in research. Emphasis is placed on character development and scene-by-scene improvisation, followed by constructive peer criticism, and a culminating performance. The play is designed for both Spanish-speaking and English-speaking students (see Appendixes A and B).

DIALOGUES OF TEACHERS AND RESEARCHERS

How does one approach the authenticity of autobiography in the writing of the life of another? So many differences in culture, language background, religious conviction, and income (to name a few) could potentially separate researchers and prevent understanding. Yet, when dialogic teacher researchers approach their writing of a life as a dialogue in search of common ground—as parents, as educators, as Americans—the authenticity would arise from their dialogues together.

Dialogic teacher researchers show their value for the relationship that they establish with informants by respecting their words, their interpretations, and their theories. In this way, researchers have the opportunity to reexamine their own theories as well as their own voice. By sharing drafts of their work with family participants, researchers are able to clarify words, themes, and theories, as well as get a sense of the respect that participants have for the sharing of stories, and for passing along these stories to a wider audience.

Researchers must also learn to value the artistry in the voice of the informant, and to show that value in the way that they represent voices of others in the content and form of the text. The narratives in this volume bring the vitality and the aesthetic quality of oral accounts into the written form. Brunner (1994) has called for such a return to the aesthetic: "We need a new vision, and I believe as others that part of that vision can occur through the systematic use of aesthetic materials—materials that allow for an opening onto educational theory, social theory, and critical practice, materials that allow for imagining our world as it could be otherwise" (p. 236). Researchers who wish to add authenticity to their work and broaden its scope and audience should consider alternatives to the dry prose of many social science texts, which squeeze the life out of words.

Through this research, the voices of refugee and immigrant families can be brought into the public discourse about education. Of course, such an approach to educational life history could also be of research relevance to other people in American society whose voices need to be heard. Lincoln (1993) suggested that by writing narratives of the *silenced*, new avenues can be opened for social scientists. The study of lives can lead to developments in grounded theories. Moreover, by including the protagonists in the construction of their own narratives, narrative inquirers can gain multivocality and authority of voice. Such multivocality is needed in educational circles, as many teachers and policymakers have little personal experience of the daily struggle faced by poor students and their families, and the voices of such families and students are rarely heard when educational policy is being formulated. Narratives have the power to bring these voices to the attention of educators and policymakers.

Teachers can draw on the cultural resources of parents and students, thereby enriching the curriculum and school life. Moll and Greenberg (1990) showed that extending the "zones of knowledge" from the school into families and communities has definite implications for curriculum and instruction. In their view, the immigrant home can and should be a locus for action research by teaching professionals. By examining the learning taking place in the home, teachers can challenge common assumptions about "cultural deficits."

Teacher education must not only expose preservice and continuing teachers to the lives of refugees and immigrants, but must provide them with the conceptual and methodological tools to better understand those lives. Principles and practice of ethnographic and narrative inquiry should be a part of teacher preparation programs. As suggested by Zeichner (1993), preservice teachers should be encouraged to address their own sense of cultural identity as well as participate in direct intercultural experiences in the wider community. The use of ethnographic techniques such as participant observation and field notes can help students document these experiences for later reflection with colleagues (Moll, 1992).

Witherell and Noddings (1991) suggested that narratives are central to the work of teachers and counselors, allowing one to penetrate cultural barriers, discover one's "self" and the "other," and deepen understanding. Critically examining the autobiographies of immigrants and their children within the context of a discussion group is one promising way of increasing the cultural understanding of teachers from both majority and minority cultures (Florio-Ruane & DeTar, 1995; Galindo & Olguin, 1996).

Finally, a better understanding of the lives of refugees and immigrants questions forces teachers, researchers and educators to raise critical questions: Why are immigrants and refugees here in the first place? What responsibility does the American government and society have for refugees and immigrants, many of whom are here as a direct result of American military and economic activity abroad? As educators of all children, what responsibility do schools have for reaching out to all parents, especially those who do not speak the dominant language? Why is there so little room for other languages in public schools in our country? How should schools prepare the next generation of citizens for America and the world? Good narratives cause the reader to ask such moral questions. They en-able educators to engage students and others in the "realm of practical ethics" on the mutual "quest for goodness and meaning" (Witherell & Noddings, 1991, p. 4).

SCHOOL AND COMMUNITY DIALOGUE

There is much that can be done to promote dialogue between schools and refugee and immigrant communities. Certainly, school districts can make better efforts to invite families and community members into the schools, to share their skills in classrooms, and to participate in community activity nights. During the past school year in Oshkosh, there have been "Parent Community Nights" on most Fridays. Families of children in the ESL program come to share a meal and a variety of activities: There are games, art, and story reading for the children, movies, basketball in the gym, cooking lessons for a variety of international cuisines, ESL for adults, and Hmong language and literacy lessons for Hmong children and youth.

Bilingual community liaisons provide unique channels dialogue between homes and schools. A model for the use of these liaisons can be found at the Center for Language, Culture and the Communication Arts (CLCCA) a focus school within the Lansing, Michigan school district. A school brochure states that "the CLCCA promotes a positive international, interethnic and interracial climate by identifying, sharing and supporting cultural values from our Global Learning Community." A majority of the approximately 300 students at the school come from families that have recently immigrated from places such as Laos, Vietnam, Iraq, Mexico, and Haiti. Ninety percent of the students speak a first language other than English. Families choose to send children to the CLCCA because the school explicitly values diverse languages and cultures and encourages an ongoing dialogue between the school and linguistic minority communities. School staff and children regularly participate in city-wide educational conferences and cultural festivals. The CLCCA also publishes and disseminates various materials, including a booklet on cultural traditions, whose writers included refugee children and parents, teachers, the principal, the mayor of Lansing, and the president of Michigan State University. Sharon Peck, principal at the CLCCA, describes the role of the school as an "ingathering" of children from diverse cultures and an "outflowing" of cultural and linguistic information to the entire community. She also suggests that the role played by the bilingual community liaisons is fundamental:

> The community liaison's role is so critical. They are the diplomatic corps, the glue, that has always been such an integral part of this type of program. Not only because of the legal aspect of having kids work with adults who speak their own language. Even if it weren't for that, it wouldn't make sense to run

the program without their involvement. I'm not Hmong, and Yvonne's not Vietnamese or Laotian, and we don't know what we are talking about when it comes to defining critical elements in the families' lives, and their language, and what is meaningful and not meaningful for them. Insofar as having a certified teacher legitimizes what is going on in the classroom, having people that speak all the languages of the kids who study here, legitimizes this effort in the eyes of parents. (Hones, 1999, p. 150)

The work of the community liaisons, in this sense, mirrors the use of bilingual staff at Leonard Covello's (1958) community centered school in East Harlem:

We were not separate, off somewhere in a world of our own, unapproachable to the man, woman or child who could not speak English. How often have I seen the lightning joy on the face of a dubious immigrant parent when he hears the sound of a familiar tongue! How many barriers crumble before the shared language! (pp. 266–267)

Bilingual community liaisons are the interpreters and bearers of information between distinct communities and worldviews. They help make possible relationships between school and community that are not based on a common language or understanding of the world, but on trust.

This year in our dialogic teacher research, we will be producing texts specifically for immigrant and refugee families. One project involves the collection of family stories by researchers and the creation and publication of bilingual family storybooks, with pictures, photos and basic literacy in two languages. These books will provide a family record of their lives, as well as offer literacy opportunities for children and adults alike.

In a second project, teacher researchers are familiarized with the legal rights of English language learners, including the right to comprehensible materials and instruction, parental involvement in special education decisions, and high academic expectations for all students by teachers, counselors, and principals. Teacher researchers then create bilingual storybooks for immigrant and refugee families on the rights of their children to a quality education. With a simple, bilingual text, and many photos and pictures, these books can serve as adult literacy tools for parents, while teaching them about the nature of the American school system and their children's rights to a quality, comprehensible education.

DIALOGUES ACROSS BORDERS

Dialogic teacher research, where the linguistic and cultural understandings of immigrants and refugees are sources of knowledge creation and bridges to the curriculum, will benefit bilingual students academically and socially. This research has the potential to transform the lives of bilingual students and those who work with them. When engaged in dialogues with teachers about critical perspectives on language, culture, history, and other subjects, refugee and immigrant families become more interested in the work of school and more motivated to master the linguistic tools that will allow them to fully experience their economic, social, cultural and political rights.

Flecha (1999) argued that "educational and social failure (of marginalized youth) is the failure of an educational system and a society that can neither recognize nor make use of the cultural richness of different groups and individuals" (p. 78). Rather, schools can be "public spheres, actively engaged in producing new forms of democratic community organized as sites of translation, negotiation, and resistance" (p. 111). From school textbooks to Hollywood movies, most students continue to come across a version of America where White American values and heroes comprise the dominant worldviews of our times. When educators challenge this dominant perspective and encourage the development of students' own stories and perspectives of the world, they take on the role of *border crossers* (Giroux, 1997). The border crosser commits him or herself to remembering and to helping students to remember their own histories of struggle; to value diverse cultural and linguistic understandings of the world; and to prepare students with the critical tools to address the unequal distribution of power in society. Strategically placed between the home, the school, and society, educators have sometimes exacerbated cultural conflicts in students' lives, yet they are also in a position to do the work of cultural healing that is necessary in our often-wounded society. Through the use of dialogic pedagogy and as producers of culture, educators can encourage students to create knowledge and to critically address unequal power constructions in their lives.

This is the particular challenge facing educators and policymakers working in the culturally and linguistically rich America of the new millennium: to help develop the academic, cultural and social skills students will need, not to assimilate to a "Madison Avenue culture" in crisis, but to effectively struggle for, and bring into being, a new democratic culture. Such a culture will value people, and their diverse ideas and contributions, rather than profits. Such a culture will give credence to hopes and dreams of freedom, equality, and brotherhood.

The "Bully 4-U!" Award

This dramatic piece helps teachers and students think about the contrast between the behavior that is awarded in school and that is awarded in the global economy. Billy Gried, this year's winner of the "Bully 4-U" award, is honored for his example in putting together a thriving Pokémon card business that employs 5 people, generates significant income for investment, and allows Billy to give something back to the community (starter Pokémon sets for toddlers). Billy is asked to describe his experiences by an admiring principal and audience. He talks of starting out with a sizable Pokémon set of his own, and making trades, discarding his duplicates and gaining cards that were of value. On occasion, when students were unwilling to trade complete sets that he needed, Oscar, his chief employee, would "lean on them a little" until they gave up the cards for free. Billy also managed to start selling duplicates to younger children, first making them understand that the Pokémon were essential for life. This was made easier, he explains, because the mass media had already done the job for him. Children would give Billy their lunch money for cards, and this money he invested, and turned a considerable profit. He has also hired several of these children, who are now working for food, to be distributors for him at other neighborhoods in the area. Billy asked Oscar to also work for food, but Oscar refused, insisting on his usual cash payment. "So, I had to let him go," Billy explains. Oscar now menaces the smaller children who have replaced him, so they try to do their distributing after dark. Finally, Billy is proud to announce that, because his earnings are extensive, he is able to put something back into the community, and is now providing selected underprivileged toddlers with starter Pokémon cards.

On the completion of this dramatized award ceremony, children in the audience are asked what they think about Billy receiving an award for this kind of behavior. Do they think adults, or nations, should be rewarded for

171

this kind of behavior? Yet, it is this behavior that is rewarded in the global economy, and has helped build the United States into a global economic and political power. The specific history of United States–Mexican relations is highlighted, including Mexico's loss of half of its national territory between 1835 and 1848, and U.S. influence on its economy and the working lives of many Mexican people.

*Escuche Bien, Amigo**

Characters:

Scroggins, a teacher
Lupe, a student
Maria, her little sister
Clinton, her little brother
Magdalena, her mother
La Lucha
Joe, an ex-farmer
The supervisor
Subcomandante Marcos
Zapatista guerilla
Soldier(s)
Banker (Chase)
General
President of the United States
President of Mexico
Mother
Father
Child
Hawkers

Scene One:

Scroggins, exhausted from a day of teaching his students, many who are recent arrivals from Mexico, falls asleep at his desk. He is awakened by La Lucha, the spirit of struggle, a mysterious visitor. She asks him what is bothering him and he says, "My students just don't get it." She says, *"Es*

---

posible que tu no lo entiendes," ["Maybe it's you who doesn't understand"] and she then suggests that they could take a little trip to find out about this.

Scene Two:

Scroggins and Lucha at Lupe's house. There is no heat, and it is quite cold indoors. The parents are at work. Lupe is trying to prepare food for the smaller children, and playing a game of "circus" under a big blanket with them, to help them forget the cold. Scroggins wonders where the parents are, and why don't they ever come to parent teacher conferences, anyway? Lucha suggests they can go find out.

Scene Three:

At the packing plant where Lupe's parents both work. The stench is incredible, guts are all over the floor, and parts of cows hang from the rafters. Magdalena, the children's mother, is cutting into the raw meat with saws. Next to her is Joe, who grew up on a farm nearby. They talk about the farming life they have had and lost. The supervisor comes through and tells them they will have to speed things up. Scroggins says, they don't seem so bad off, at least she has a job, she seems grateful. But where is their father, anyway? Lucha says to him, *"Todavia, no lo entiendes, ¿verdad?"* ["You still don't get it, do you?"] and beckons him to come.

Scene Four:

San Cristobal de Las Casas, New Years Day, 1994. Subcomandante Marcos is talking to the press about the Zapatistas, their opposition to NAFTA, and their goals for the region and for Mexico. Scroggins listens and says he can appreciate the ideas, but what do they need guns for? They don't seem to trust their own government, let alone the Americans. Lucha smiles and leads him on.

Scene Five:

Washington, DC, early 1995. The presidents of the United States and Mexico, a general, and a banker from Chase Manhattan are gathered. The banker warns them that "the Zapatistas must be eliminated" or investors would not take a chance on Mexico. The president of Mexico asks for help, and the general offers equipment. The U.S. president stipulates that the military equipment is intended for the "war on drugs," but indicates that he believes that there are drugs in Chiapas, as well. The general also suggests to the president of Mexico that he send more of his officers for special training in counterinsurgency at the School of the Americas in Georgia. Scroggins can't quite figure it out—what are they planning? Shouldn't the American people know about this? Lucha leads him on.

Scene Six:

A jungle village in Chiapas. Soldiers are carrying out a "low intensity warfare" campaign against Zapatista base communities: Villagers are ordered out under pain of death, then the villages is burned down, the wells poisoned, and the crops destroyed. The soldiers take several adults in for "questioning," including one child's father ... The child cries out, *"No te olvido, papa ... "* ["I won't forget you, Dad"] Scroggins can't believe the brutality of the soldiers and the desperation of the survivors. Who told them to do this? He wonders. Lucha reminds him of the Chase memo, that the Zapatistas must be eliminated to encourage investment. She leads him on.

Scene Seven:

A street in Tijuana, Mexico. Hawkers try to sell margaritas, girls, etcetera. to Scroggins, who waves them off. He sees small children and their impoverished mothers begging on the bridge between the United States and Mexico, with the children wailing out *cielito lindo* for the tourists. Scroggins approaches one of the young women for sale along la *Avenida de la Revolucion* ... he sees his own daughter, shouts, and reaches out for her, but the girl backs away, and he is hit over the head ....

Scene Eight:

Scroggins wakes up at school, finds his daughter safe. He begins to talk with his students about their lives and their reasons for coming to the United States. Outside they here marchers coming down the street: Magdalena, Lupe's mother, and Joe are leading a group of workers from the packing plant who have gone on strike. Scroggins and his entire class join them in the street, where chants are heard: "The people, united, will never be defeated/*El pueblo, unido, jamas sera vencido."*

This improvisational theater was first performed at the International TESOL Convention in St. Louis, Missouri, on March 1, 2001.

References

Andrade, R. (1998). Life in elementary school: Children's ethnographic reflections. In A. Egan-Robertson & D. Bloome (Eds.), *Students as researchers of culture and language in their own communities* (pp. 93–114). New York: Hampton Press.

Anyon, J. (1995). Race, social class, and educational reform in an inner-city school. *Teachers College Record, 97*(1), 69–94.

Ashabranner, B. (1987). *The vanishing border*. New York: Dodd.

Atrocities and the Humanitarian Crisis in Kosovo. (1999). Hearing before the Commission on Security and Cooperation in Europe: One hundred sixth congress, first session (CSCE 106, 1–4).Washington, DC: U.S. Government Printing Office.

Ayers, W. (1989). *The good preschool teacher: Six teachers reflect on their lives*. New York: Teachers College Press.

Bakhtin, M. (1981). *The dialogic imagination*. Austin: University of Texas Press.

Barone, T. (1995). Persuasive writings, vigilant readings, and reconstructed characters: The paradox of trust in educational storysharing. In J. Hatch & R. Wisniewski (Eds.), *Life history and narrative* (pp. 63–74). Bristol, PA: Falmer Press.

Bateson, M. (1990). *Composing a life*. New York: Plume/Penguin.

Becker, H. (1970). *Sociological work*. Chicago: Aldine.

Bellah, R., Madsen, R., Sullivan, W., Swidler, A., & Tipton, S. (1985). *Habits of the heart: Individualism and commitment in American life*. New York: Harper & Row.

Bloom, A. (1987). *The closing of the American mind*. New York: Simon & Schuster.

Bourdieu, P. (1977). Cultural reproduction and social reproduction. In J. Karabel & A. Halsey (Eds.), *Power and ideology in education* (pp. 487–511). New York: Oxford University Press.

Brisk, M. E. (1998). *Bilingual education: From compensatory to quality schooling*. Mahwah, NJ: Lawrence Erlbaum Associates.

Brogan, P. (1989). *World conflicts*. London: Bloomsbury.

Brown, D. (1970). *Bury my heart at wounded knee: An Indian history of the American west*. New York: Bantam.

Bruner, J. (1990). *Acts of meaning*. Cambridge, MA: Harvard University Press.

Brunner, D. (1994). *Inquiry and reflection: Framing narrative practice in education.* Albany: SUNY Press.

Brutt-Griffler, J., & Samimy, K. (1999). Revisiting the colonial in the postcolonial: Critical praxis for nonnative English-speaking teachers in a TESOL program. *TESOL Quarterly, 33*(3), 413–432.

Butt, R., Raymond, D., McCue, G., & Yamagishi, L. (1992). Collaborative autobiography and the teacher's voice. In I. Goodson (Ed.), *Studying teachers' lives,* (pp. 51–98). New York: Teachers College Press.

Campbell, G. (1999). *The road to Kosovo: A Balkan diary.* Boulder, CO: Westview Press.

Carger, C. (1996). *Of borders and dreams: A Mexican-American experience of urban education.* New York: Teachers College Press.

Carlson, D. (1996). *Making progress: Education and culture in new times.* New York: Teachers College Press.

Casey, K. (1995). The new narrative research in education. In M. Apple (Ed.), *Review of research in education, 1995–1996* (pp. 211–254). Washington, DC: American Education/Research Association.

Chomsky, N. (1994). Time bombs. In E. Katzenberger (Ed.), *First world, ha ha ha: The Zapatista challenge.* San Francisco: City Lights.

Clandinin, D., & Connelly, F. (1994). Personal experience methods. In N. Denzin & Y. Lincoln (Eds.), *Handbook of qualitative research* (pp. 413–547). Thousand Oaks, CA: Sage.

Clausen, J. (1993). *American lives: Looking back at children of the Great Depression.* New York: Free Press.

Cochran-Smith, M. (1995). Color blindness and basket making are not the answers: Confronting the dilemmas of race, culture, and language diversity in teacher education. *American Educational Research Journal 32*(3), 493–523.

Cooper, R. (1986). The Hmong of Laos: Economic factors in the refugee exodus and return. In G. Hendricks, B. Downing, & A. Deinard (Eds.), *The Hmong in Transition* (pp. 23–40). New York: The Center for Migration Studies.

Covello, L. (1958). *The heart is the teacher.* New York: McGraw-Hill.

Crapanzano, V. (1980). *Tuhami: Portrait of a Moroccan.* Chicago: University of Chicago Press.

Cremin, L. (1988). *American education: The metropolitan experience, 1876–1980.* New York: Harper & Row.

Cummins, J. (1994). Knowledge, power, and identity in teaching English as a second language. In F. Genesee (Ed.), *Educating second language children: The whole child, the whole curriculum, the whole community* (pp. 33–58). New York: Cambridge University Press.

Delgado-Gaitan, C. (1996). *Protean literacy: Extending the discourse on empowerment.* Bristol, PA: Falmer Press.

Delgado-Gaitan, C., & Trueba, H. (1991). *Crossing cultural borders: Education for immigrant families in America.* New York: Falmer Press.

Delpit, L. (1987). Power and pedagogy in educating other people's children. *Harvard Educational Review, 58*(3), 280–298.

Denzin, N. (1994). The art and politics of interpretation. In N. Denzin & Y. Lincoln (Eds.), *Handbook of qualitative research* (pp. 500–515). Thousand Oaks, CA: Sage.

Dunnigan, T. (1986). Processes of identity maintenance in Hmong society. In G. Hendricks, B. Downing, & A. Deinard (Eds.), *The Hmong in transition* (pp. 41–54). New York: The Center for Migration Studies.

Ebert, K. (1997, March 31). Worlds away: Family takes Oshkosh culture. *Oshkosh Northwestern*, Sec. 1: 1.

Entesser, N. (1992). *Kurdish nationalism*. Boulder, CO: Lynne Reinner.

Entwistle, H. (1977). *Class, culture, and education*. London: Methuen.

Erikson, E. (1950). *Childhood and society*. New York: Norton.

Flecha, R. (1999). New educational inequalities. In M. Castells, R. Flecha, P. Freire, H. Giroux, D. Macedo, & P. Willis (Eds.), *Critical education in the new information age* (pp. 65–82). Lanham, MD: Rowman & Littlefield.

Florio-Ruane, S., & DeTar, J. (1995). Conflict and consensus in teacher candidates' discussion of ethnic autobiography. *English Education, 27*(1), 11–39.

Foley, D. (1996). The silent Indian as a cultural production. In B. Levinson, D. Foley, & D. Holland (Eds.), *The cultural production of the educated person: Critical ethnographies of schooling and local practice* (pp. 79–92). Albany, NY: SUNY Press.

Foster, M. (1993). Self-portraits of Black teachers: Narratives of individual and collective struggle against racism. In D. McLaughlin & W. Tierney (Eds.), *Naming silenced lives: Personal narratives and processes of educational change* (pp. 155–176). New York: Routledge.

Freire, P. (1970). *Pedagogy of the oppressed*. New York: Herder & Herder.

Freire, P. (1971). *Sobre la Accion Cultural* [Concerning cultural action]. Santiago, Chile: ICIRA.

Freire, P. (1998). *Pedagogy of freedom: Ethics, democracy, and civic courage*. Lanham, MA: Rowman & Littlefield.

Frye, D. (1999). Participatory education as a critical framework for an immigrant women's ESL class. *TESOL Quarterly, 33*(3), 501–512.

Fuchs, L. (1990). *The American kaleidoscope: Race, ethnicity, and the civic culture*. Hanover, NH: Wesleyan University Press.

Galindo, R., & Olguin, M. (1996). Reclaiming bilingual educators' cultural resources: An autobiographical approach. *Urban Education, 31*(1), 29–56.

Gee, J. (1990). *Social linguistics and literacies: Ideology in discourses*. Philadelphia: Falmer Press.

Geertz, C. (1987). Notes on a Balinese cockfight. In P. Rabinow & W. Sullivan (Eds.), *Interpretive social science: A second look* (pp. 195–240). Berkeley: University of California Press.

Ghassemlou, A. (1980). *People without a country: The Kurds and Kurdistan*. London: Zed Press.

Gibson, M. (1988). *Adaptation without assimilation: Sikh immigrants in an American high school*. Ithaca, NY: Cornell University Press.

Gibson, M. (1998). Promoting academic success among immigrant students: Is acculturation the issue? *Educational Policy, 12*(6), 615–633.

Giroux, H. (1996). Doing cultural studies: Youth and the challenge of pedagogy. In P. Leistyna, A. Woodrum, & S. Sherblom (Eds.), *Breaking free: The transformative power of critical pedagogy* (pp. 83–108). Cambridge, MA: Harvard University Press.

Giroux, H. (1997). *Pedagogy and the politics of hope: Theory, culture and schooling.* Boulder, CO: Westview.

Giroux, H., Lankshear, C., McLaren, P., & Peters, M. (1996). *Counternarratives: Cultural studies and critical pedagogies in postmodern spaces.* New York: Routledge.

Gitlin, A., & Meyers, B. (1993). Beth's story: The search for a mother/teacher. In D. McLaughlin & W. Tierney (Eds.), *Naming silenced lives: Personal narratives and processes of educational change* (pp. 51–70). New York: Routledge.

Goodlad, J. (1984). *A place called school: Prospects for the future.* New York: McGraw-Hill.

Goodson, I. (1992). Studying teachers' lives: An emergent field of inquiry. In I. Goodson (Ed.), *Studying teachers' lives* (pp. 1–17). New York: Teachers College Press.

Goodson, I., & Cole, A. (1993). Exploring the teacher's professional knowledge. In D. McLaughlin & W. Tierney (Eds.), *Naming silenced lives: Personal narratives and processes of educational change* (pp. 71–94). New York: Routledge.

Greene, M. (1996). In search of a critical pedagogy. In P. Leistyna, A. Woodrum, & S. Sherblom (Eds.), *Breaking free: The transformative power of critical pedagogy* (pp. 13–30). Cambridge, MA: Harvard University Press.

Grinberg, J., & Goldfarb, K. P. (1998). Moving teacher education into the community. *Theory into Practice, 37*(2), 131–139.

Grumet, M. (1991). The politics of personal knowledge. In C. Witherell & N. Noddings (Eds.), *Stories lives tell: Narrative and dialogue in education* (pp. 67–77). New York: Teachers College Press.

Gunter, M. (1992). *The Kurds of Iraq: Tragedy and hope.* New York: St. Martin's Press.

Gunter, M. (1999). *The Kurdish predicament in Iraq: A Political Analysis.* New York: St. Martin's Press.

Gutierrez, D. (1996). *Between two worlds: Mexican immigrants in the United States.* Wilmington, DE: Scholarly Resources.

Hamilton-Merritt, J. (1993). *Tragic mountains: The Hmong, the Americans, and the secret wars for Laos, 1942–1992.* Bloomington, IN: Indiana University Press.

Hauser, M. (1994). Working with school staff: "Reflective cultural analysis" in groups. In G. Spindler & L. Spindler (Eds.), *Pathways to cultural awareness: Cultural therapy with teachers and students* (pp. 169–195). Newbury Park, CA: Corwin Press.

Heath, S. (1983). *Ways with words.* New York: Cambridge University Press.

Hilsman, R. (1992). *George Bush vs. Saddam Hussein.* Novato, CA: Presido Press.

Hirsch, E. (1988). *Cultural literacy: What every American needs to know.* New York: Vintage.

Hirst, D. (1996, December 15). Kurds trapped between Iraqi army terror and winter's fury. *Manchester Guardian Weekly,* p. 11.

Hones, D. (1993). In the spirit of Evaristo: Using improvisational theater with EFL students in Ecuador. *Language Quarterly, 30*(3–4), 42–46.

Hones, D. (1999). U.S. justice? Critical pedagogy and the case of Mumia Abu-Jamal. *TESOL Journal 8*(4), 27–33.

Hones, D., & Cha, C. S. (1999). *Educating new Americans: Immigrant lives and learning.* Mahwah, NJ: Lawrence Erlbaum Associates.

Honig, J., & Botha, N. (1996). *Srebrenica: A record of a war crime.* New York: Penguin.

Horton, M. (1990). *The long haul.* New York: Doubleday.

Jacques, E. (1995). *The Albanians: An ethnic history from prehistoric times to the present.* London: McFarland & Company, Inc.

Jencks, R. (1994). *Insurgency and social disorder in Guizhou: The "Miao" Rebellion, 1854–1873.* Honolulu: University of Hawaii Press.

Kiedrowski, S. (1998). *A Hmong family narrative.* Unpublished manuscript, University of Wisconsin, Oshkosh, College of Education and Human Services.

Kincheloe, J. (1993). *Toward a critical politics of teacher thinking: Mapping the postmodern.* Westport, CT: Bergin & Garvey.

Kozol, J. (1991). *Savage inequalities: Children in America's schools.* New York: Crown.

Ladson-Billings, G. (1995). Toward a theory of culturally relevant pedagogy. *American Educational Research Journal, 32*(3), 465–492.

Lawyers Committee for Human Rights. (1989). *Forced back and forgotten: The human rights of Laotian asylum seekers in Thailand.* New York: Author.

Lazarus, R. S., & Launier, R. (1978). Stress-related transactions between person and environment. In L. A. Pervin & M. Lewis (Eds.), *Perspectives in interactional psychology* (pp. 114–135). New York: Springer.

Lee, G. (1986). Culture and adaptation: Hmong refugees in Australia. In G. Hendricks, B. Downing, & A. Deinard (Eds.), *The Hmong in transition* (pp. 55–72). New York: Center for Migration Studies.

Lee, G. (1996). Cultural identity in post-modern society: Reflections on what is Hmong? *Hmong Studies Journal, 1*(2), 27–33.

Levinson, B., Foley, D., & Holland, D. (Eds.). (1996). *The cultural production of the educated person: Critical ethnographies of schooling and local practice.* Albany: SUNY Press.

Levinson, B., & Holland, D. (1996). The cultural production of the educated person: An introduction. In B. Levinson, D. Foley, & D. Holland (Eds.), *The cultural production of the educated person: Critical ethnographies of schooling and local practice* (pp. 1–54). Albany: SUNY Press.

Lewis, O. (1966). The culture of poverty. *Scientific American, 215,* 19–25.

Lincoln, Y. (1993). I and thou: Method, voice and roles in research with the silenced. In D. McLaughlin & W. Tierney (Eds.), *Naming silenced lives: Personal narratives and processes of educational change* (pp. 29–47). New York: Routledge.

Livo, N., & Cha, D. (1991). *Folk stories of the Hmong.* Englewood, CO: Libraries Unlimited.

Long, L. (1993). *Ban Vinai: The refugee camp.* New York: Columbia University Press.

Luykx, A. (1996). From *Indios* to *Profesionales* [Indians to professionals]: Stereotypes and student resistance in Bolivian teacher training. In B. Levinson, D. Foley, & D. Holland (Eds.), *The cultural production of the educated person: Critical ethnographies of schooling and local practice* (pp. 239–272). Albany: SUNY Press.

Maciel, D., & Herrera-Sobek, M. (Eds.). (1998). *Culture across borders: Mexican immigration and popular culture.* Tucson: University of Arizona Press.

Mackie, A. (1999). Possibilities for feminism in ESL education and research. *TESOL Quarterly, 33*(3), 566–572.

Mattison, W., Lo, L., & Scarseth, T. (1994). *Hmong lives.* La Crosse, WI: The Pump House.

McBeth, S., & Horne, E. (1996). "I know who I am": The collaborative life history of a Shoshone Indian woman. In G. Etter-Lewis & M. Foster (Eds.), *Unrelated kin: Race and gender in women's personal narratives.* New York: Routledge.

McCaleb, S. P. (1998). Connecting preservice teacher education to diverse communities: A focus on family literacy. *Theory into Practice, 37*(2), 148–154.

McCandless, B. R. (1952). Environment and intelligence. *American Journal of Mental Deficiency, 56,* 674–691.

McCoy, A. (1991). *The politics of heroin: CIA complicity in the global drug trade.* Brooklyn, NY: Lawrence Hill Books.

McDowall, D. (1996). *A modern history of the Kurds.* London: I.B. Tauris.

McLaren, P. (2000). *Che Guevara, Paulo Freire, and the pedagogy of revolution.* Lanham, MD: Rowman & Littlefield.

McLaughlin, D. (1993). Personal narratives of school change in Navajo settings. In D. McLaughlin & W. Tierney (Eds.), *Naming silenced lives: Personal narratives and processes of educational change* (pp. 95–118). New York: Routledge.

McLaughlin, D., & Tierney, W. (Eds.). (1993). *Naming silenced lives: Personal narratives and processes for educational change.* New York: Routledge.

Meiselas, S. (1997). *Kurdistan: In the shadow of history.* New York: Random House.

Mendoza, R. H. (1984). Acculturation and sociocultural variability. In J. L. Martinez & R. H. Mendoza (Eds.), *Chicano psychology* (2nd ed). New York: Academic Press.

Merrill, T., & Miro, R. (1997). *Mexico: A country study.* Washington, DC: Library of Congress.

Meyer, R. (1996). *Stories from the heart: Teachers and students researching their literacy lives.* Mahwah, NJ: Lawrence Erlbaum Associates.

Miller, D. (1996). "I have a frog in my stomach": Mythology and truth in life history. In G. Etter-Lewis & M. Foster (Eds.), *Unrelated kin: Race and gender in women's personal narratives* (pp. 103–121). New York: Routledge.

Mills, C. W. (1959). *The sociological imagination.* New York: Oxford University Press.

Moll, L. (1992). Bilingual classroom studies and community analysis: Some recent trends. *Educational Researcher, 3,* 20–24.

Moll, L., & Greenberg, J. (1990). Creating zones of possibilities: Combining social contexts for instruction. In L. Moll (Ed.), *Vygotsky and education: Instructional implications for applications of sociohistorical psychology* (pp. 319–348). New York: Cambridge University Press.

Moll, L., Velez-Ibañez, C., & Greenberg, J. (1989). *Year one progress report: Community knowledge and classroom practice: Combining resources for literacy instruction* (IARP Subcontract No. L-10). Washington, DC: Development Associates.

Montero-Sieburth, M., & Gray, C. (1992). Riding the wave: Collaborative inquiry linking teachers at the university and the urban high school. In C. Grant (Ed.), *Research and multicultural education: From the margins to the mainstream* (pp. 122–140). Bristol, PA: Falmer Press.

Moore, D. (1989). *Dark sky, dark land: Stories of the Hmong boy scouts of troop 100.* Eden Prairie, MN: Tessera Publishing.

Moraes, M. (1996). *Bilingual education: A dialogue with the Bakhtin circle.* Albany, NY: SUNY Press.

Narayan, R. K. (1987). The ramayana. New York: Vision Books.

National Center for Educational Statistics. (1989). Dropout rates in the United States. Washington, DC: U.S. Department of Education.

Oakes, J. (1985). *Keeping track: How schools structure inequality.* New Haven, CT: Yale University Press.

Ogbu, J. (1982). Cultural discontinuities and schooling. *Anthropology and Education Quarterly, 13*(4), 290–307.

Ogbu, J. (1991). Immigrant and involuntary minorities in comparative perspective. In M. Gibson & J. Ogbu (Eds.), *Minority status and schooling: A comparative study of immigrant and involuntary minorities* (pp. 3–36). New York: Garland.

Okihiro, G. (1994). *Margins and mainstreams: Asians in American history and culture.* Seattle: University of Washington Press.

Olmedo, I. M. (1997). Family oral histories for multicultural curriculum perspectives. *Urban Education, 32*(1), 45–62.

Padilla, A. M., Cervantes, R. C., Maldonado, M., & Garcia, R. E. (1988). Coping response to psychosocial stressors among Mexican and central American immigrants. *Journal of Community Psychology, 16,* 418–427.

Pai, Y. (1990). *Cultural foundations of education.* Columbus, OH: Merrill.

Paley, V. (1995). *Kwaanza and me.* Cambridge: Harvard University Press.

Paley, V. (1977). *White teacher.* Cambridge: Harvard University Press.

Peters, M., & Lankshear, C., (1996). Postmodern counternarratives. In H. Giroux, C. Lankshear, P. McLaren, & M. Peters (Eds.), *Counternarratives: Cultural studies and critical pedagogies in postmodern spaces* (pp. 1–40). New York: Routledge.

Pennycook, A. (1999). Introduction: Critical approaches to TESOL. *TESOL Quarterly 33*(3), 329–348.

Peyton, J. K., & Staton, J. (Eds.). (1993). *Dialogue journals in the multilingual classroom: Building language fluency and writing skills through written interaction.* Norwood, NJ: Ablex.

Phelan, P., & Davidson, A. (1994). Looking across borders: Students' investigations of family, peer, and school worlds as cultural therapy. In G. Spindler & L. Spindler (Eds.), *Pathways to cultural awareness: Cultural therapy with teachers and students* (pp. 35–59). Thousand Oaks, CA: Corwin Press.

Phillips, D. (1994). Telling it straight: Issues in assessing narrative research. *Educational Psychologist, 29*(1), 13–21.

Polkinghorne, D. (1995). Narrative configuration in qualitative analysis. In J. Hatch & R. Wisniewski (Eds.), *Life history and narrative* (pp. 5–23). Bristol, PA: Falmer.

Prifti, P. (1999). *Confrontation in Kosova: The Albanian-Serb struggle, 1969–1999.* New York: Columbia University Press.

Rabinow, P. (1977). *Reflections on fieldwork in Morocco.* Berkeley: University of California Press.

Rabinow, P., & Sullivan, W. (1987). The interpretive turn: A second look. In P. Rabinow & W. Sullivan (Eds.), *Interpretive social science: A second look* (pp. 1–30). Berkeley: University of California Press.

Ranard, D. (1989). The last bus. *Atlantic Monthly, 260*(4), 26–34.

Reed, L. (1993). Opening the door to communication in the multilingual/multicultural classroom. In J. K. Peyton & J. Staton (Eds.), *Dialogue journals in the multilingual classroom: Building language fluency and writing skills through written interaction.* Norwood, NJ: Ablex.

Richardson, L. (1992). The consequences of poetic representation: Writing the other, rewriting the self. In C. Ellis & M. Flaherty (Eds.), *Investigating subjectivity: Research on lived experience* (pp. 125–140). Newbury Park, CA: Sage.

Riding, A. (1985). *Distant neighbors.* New York: Knopf.

Rodriguez, R. (1982). *Hunger of memory: The education of Richard Rodriguez.* New York: Bantam.

Rogel, C. (1998). *The breakup of Yugoslavia and the war in Bosnia.* Westport, CT: Greenwood Press.

Ross, J. (1998). *The annexation of Mexico: From the Aztecs to the IMF.* Monroe, ME: Common Courage Press.

Sarris, G. (1993). *Keeping Slug woman alive: A holistic approach to American Indian texts.* Berkeley: University of California Press.

Schlesinger, A. (1991). *The disuniting of America.* New York: Norton.

Schulz, R. (1997). *Interpreting teacher practice ... two continuing stories.* New York: Teachers College Press.

Serrano, L., Dryer, L., Fink, A., & Cortes, M. G. (1998). *The Cortes family: An ethnographic study.* Unpublished manuscript, University of Wisconsin, Oshkosh, College of Education and Human Services.

Shah, S. (1994). Roses, rites, and racism: An interview with Sophea Mouth. In L. Aguilar-San Jan (Ed.), *The state of Asian America: Activism and resistance in the 1990s* (pp. 119–124). Boston: South End Press.

Shor, I. (1992). *Empowering education: Critical teaching for social change.* Chicago: University of Chicago Press.

Simons, G. (1994). *Iraq: From Sumer to Saddam.* New York: St. Martin's Press.

Simons, M. (2001, January 7). 'Balkan syndrome' fears increase. *New York Times,* 1.

Sinclair, U. (1906). *The jungle.* New York: Doubleday.

Sleeter, C., & Grant, C. (1991). Mapping terrains of power: Student cultural knowledge versus classroom knowledge. In C. Sleeter (Ed.), *Empowerment through multicultural education* (pp. 49–68). Albany, NY: SUNY Press.

Smith, S. (1984). *The theater arts and the teaching of languages.* New York: Addison-Wesley.

Soto, L. (1997). *Language, culture, and power: Bilingual families and the struggle for quality education*. Albany, NY: SUNY Press.

Spener, D. (1988). Transitional bilingual education and the socialization of immigrants. *Harvard Educational Review, 58*(2), 133–153.

Spindler, G., & Spindler, L. (1990). *The American cultural dialogue and its transmission*. New York: Falmer Press.

Spindler, G., & Spindler, L. (Eds.). (1994). *Pathways to cultural awareness: Cultural therapy with teachers and students*. Newbury Park, CA: Corwin Press.

Tedlock, D. (1983). *The spoken word and the work of interpretation*. Philadelphia: University of Pennsylvania Press.

Terkel, S. (1972). *Working*. New York: Avon.

Thompson, A. (1998). *A better place for them: A Hmong family narrative*. Unpublished manuscript, University of Wisconsin, Oshkosh, College of Education and Human Services.

Timmerman, K. (1992). *The death lobby: How the West armed Iraq*. London: Fourth Estate.

Tollefson, J. (1989). *Alien winds: The Reeducation of America's Indochinese refugees*. New York: Praeger.

Trueba, H. (1994). Foreword. In G. Spindler & L. Spindler (Eds.), *Pathways to cultural awareness: Cultural therapy with teachers and students* (pp. vii–xi). Thousand Oaks, CA: Corwin Press.

Trueba, H. (1998). Mexican immigrants from El Rincon: A case study of resilience and empowerment. *TESOL Journal 7*(1), 12–17.

Trueba, H., & Delgado-Gaitan, C. (Eds.). (1988). *School and society: Learning content through culture*. New York: Praeger.

Trueba, H., Jacobs, L., & Kirton, E. (1990). *Cultural conflict and adaptation: The case of Hmong children in American society*. New York: Falmer Press.

Trueba, H., & Zou, Y. (1994). *Power in education: The case of Miao University students and its significance for American culture*. Washington, DC: Falmer.

Trujillo, A. (1996). In search of Aztlan: Movimiento [movement] ideology and the creation of a Chicano worldview through schooling. In B. Levinson, D. Foley, & D. Holland (Eds.), *The cultural production of the educated person: Critical ethnographies of schooling and local practice* (pp. 119–149). Albany: SUNY Press.

Tyack, D., & Hansot, E. (1982). *Managers of virtue: Public school leadership in America, 1820–1980*. New York: Basic Books.

Urrea, L. (1993). *Across the wire*. New York: Bantam.

Urrea, L. (1996). *By the lake of sleeping children*. New York: Bantam.

U.S. Congress. (1968, January 2). *Congressional Record* (Section 702 of Public Law 90–2457, Bilingual Education Act). Washington, DC: Author.

Valdes, G. (1996). *Con respeto [with respect]: Bridging the distances between culturally diverse families and schools*. New York: Teachers College Press.

Van Damme, F. (1998). *The story of a Hmong refugee*. Unpublished manuscript, University of Wisconsin, Oshkosh, College of Education and Human Services.

Vang, C., Robinson, M., & Smith, E. (1998). *A narrative study of the Thao family*. Unpublished manuscript, University of Wisconsin, Oshkosh, College of Education and Human Services.

Vygotsky, L. (1978). *Mind in society: Development of higher psychological processes*. Cambridge: Harvard University Press.

Walker-Moffat, W. (1995). *The other side of the Asian American success story*. San Francisco: Jossey Bass.

Wasley, P. (1994). *Stirring the chalkdust: Tales of teachers changing classroom practice*. New York: Teachers College Press.

Wessels, C. (1987). *Drama*. Oxford University Press.

White, R. (1952). *Lives in progress*. New York: Dryden.

Wink, J. (2000). *Critical pedagogy: Notes from the real world*. New York: Longman.

Witherell, C., & Noddings, N. (Eds.). (1991). *Stories lives tell: Narrative and dialogue in education*. New York: Teachers College Press.

Zeichner, K. (1993). *Educating teachers for cultural diversity* (NCRTL Special Rep.). East Lansing: National Center for Research on Teacher Learning, Michigan State University.

Web Site References

Albanian history. (1998). Albanian.com. Retrieved from http://www.albanian.com/main/history/index.html

Albanian language education in Kosova: Letter sent from Abdyl Ramaj, Secretary of the ommission for Education of Democratic League of Kosova, and Head of Parliamentary Commission for Education, Science, Culture and Sports of Kosova to Frederico Mayor, UNESCO General Director, as well as to several embassies in Belgrade. Alb-net.com. Retrieved August 12, 1997 from www.alb-net.com/freekosova/education/index.htm

Allied base in north Iraq moved to Turkey. Nando net 1996 [Online. Internet]. Retrieved March 26, 1999, from http://www.nando.net/newsroom/nt/903base.html

Amnesty International. (2000). *New Amnesty International Report says NATO committed war crime during Kosovo conflict*. Retrieved from http://www.amnesty-usa.org/group/balkans/ref8.html

Assyria. *The Catholic Encyclopedia* [Online. Internet]. Retrieved March 26, 1999, from http://www.knight.org/advent/cathen/02007c.htm

Assyria [Online. Internet]. Retrieved February 26, 1999, from http://www.engr.ucdavis.edu/otamrazpauline

Assyrians. Distributed by the Assyrian representative of Sweden at the fourth World Conference on Women and NGO (Non-Governmental Organizations) Forum, China, 1995 [Online. Internet]. Retrieved March 1, 1999 from http://www.nineveh.com

Balkan Wars. (2000). *Encyclopœdia Britannica*. Retrieved from http://www.britannica.com/bcom/eb/article/4/0,5716,12124+1+11972,00.html?query=balkan%20wars, also http://www.britannica.com/bcom/eb/article/8/0,5716,47188+1+46112,00.html?query=kossovo%20polje

Cases of Kurdish attacks upon Assyrians of North Iraq [Online. Internet]. Retrieved March 26, 1999, from http://www.aina.org/cases.htm

Clark, R. (2000, January 26). *Report to UN Security Council, re: Iraq.* Retrieved from http://www.iacenter.org/rc12600.htm

Efty, A. (1996, September 3). A close-up: Internal quarrels often keep kurds from unified stand. *The Seattle Times* [Online. Internet]. Retrieved February 21, 1999, from http:// www.seattletimes.com/extra/browse/html/kurd-090396.html

The Frosina Information Network (1998). *A Frosina infobit: The Battle of Kosova (1389).* Retrieved April 1998 from http://www.frosina.org/infobits/ kosova13.shtml

The Frosina Information Network. (1996). *Albania and the Albanians.* Retrieved May 1996, from http://www.frosina.org/infobits/advmay96.shtml

Genocides against the Assyrian nation. Compiled by staff of Ashurbanipal Library and updated by Assyrian Academic Society [Online. Internet]. Retrieved March 1, 1999, from http://www.aina.org/martyr.htm

Graham-Brown, S. (1995). *The Middle East: The Kurds—A regional issue.* Writenet Country Papers (December 1995) [Online. Internet]. Retrieved February 10, 1999, from http://www.unhcr.ch/refworld/country/writenet/wrikurd.htm

Hanna, G. (1998, December). The Chaldean Assyrians under the Arab Baath regime of Iraq. *al-Muntada* [Online. Internet]. Retrieved March 1, 1999, from http://www.jps.net/ghanna/Banipal/muntada=12

Human Rights Watch. (2000, October). *Municipal elections in Kosovo.* Retrieved from http://www.hrw.org

Impressions from Iraq [Online. Internet]. Retrieved March 26, 1999, from http://www.users.cloud9.net/critique/israel-watch/Impressions.htm

Juka, S. S. *Kosova: The Albanians in Yugoslavia in light of historical documents.* Retrieved from http://www.alb-net.com/juka2.htm

Kosovo Battle: Excerpts from different encyclopediae. Srpska Mreza, 1996–2000. Retrieved from http://www.srpska-mreza.com/

Kurdish dispute has long festered in the region (1996, September 3). *USA Today,* 3 [Online. Internet.] Retrieved February 10, 1999, from http://www.usatoday.com/news/index/iraq/nirq009.htm

Marcos, S. (2000). *Comunicados de Subcomandante Insurgented Marcos* [messages from subcommandant Marcos]. Retrieved from http://members.nbci.com/ezln1/comusep2.htm

Martinez, C., & Gonzales, M. V. (2001). *Lucha libre (free fight): Superbarrio.* Retrieved from http://www.igc.org/deepdish/select/barrio.html

McCormack, S., & Pounds, T. (1997, April). Out of Iraq: Teams evacuate 6700. *State Magazine: Feature Story* [Online. Internet]. Retrieved March 30, 1999, from http://www.state.gov/www/publicati ... temag/statemag_april/feature7.html

Ramaj, A. (1997). *Albanian language education in Kosova: Letter sent from Abdyl Ramaj, Secretary of the Commission for Education of Democratic League of Kosova, and Head of Parliamentary Commission for Education, Science, Culture and Sports of Kosova to Frederico Mayor UNESCO General Director, as well as to several embassies in Belgrade.* Alb-net.com. Retrieved August 12, 1997, from, http://www.alb-net.com/freekosova/education/index.htm

Red Mexicana de Accion Frente al Libre Comercio [The Mexican Action Network on Free Trade]. NAFTA and the Mexican Economy. Retrieved from http://www.igc.org/dgap/malecon.html

Ritchie, B. (1996, June). Air Force news: Provide comfort continues in northern Iraq [Online. Internet]. Retrieved March 26, 1999, from http://www.af.mil/news/jun1996/n19960620_960585.html

Students Independent Union of the University of Prishtina. Bujar Dugolli, President of the Students Independent Union of the University of Prishtina. Retrieved September 22, 1997, from http://www.informatik.tu-muenchen.de/~januzaj/uni-prishtina/monitor_e.html

UNHCR (United Nations High Commission for Refugees). (1996, September). *Background paper on Iraqi refugees and asylum seekers*. Geneva: Centre for Documentation and Research [Online. Internet]. Retrieved February 21, 1999, from http://www.unhcr.ch/refworld/country/cdr/cdriq2.htm

UNPO (Unrepresented Nations and Peoples Organization). Kurdistan (Iraq) [Online. Internet]. Retrieved March 1, 1999, from http://www.unpo.org/member/kurdiraq/kurdiraq.html

U.S. Bureau of the Census. (2000). *Supplementary data sets*. Retrieved from http://factfinder.census.gov

Waller, D. (1995, March, 27). Iraq: Where feud and folly rule. *Time, 145*(3), 3pp. [Online. Internet]. Retrieved February 10, 1999, from http:/cgi.pathfinder.com/time/mag ... chive/1995/950327/950327.iraq.html

Willson, B. (2000). *Mexico: The slippery slope*. Retrieved from http://www.globalexchange.org/campaigns/mexico/slope

Zakho. *Catholic Encyclopedia* [Online. Internet]. Retrieved March 30, 1999, from http://www.knight.org/advent/cathen/15745c.htm

Author Index

A

Allison, C., 124
Amnesty International, 124, 147
Andrade, R., 21
Anyon, J., 10
Anzulovic, B., 146
Aronowitz, S., 162
Ashabranner, B., 70
Ayers, W., 7, 14, 22

B

Bakhtin, M., 5
Barone, T., 7, 15
Bateson, M., 7
Becker, H., 6
Bellah, R., 6
Bennett, C., 146
Bereiter, C., 20
Bloom, A., 16, 22
Botha, N., 146
Bourdieu, P., 13
Bringa, T., 146
Brisk, M. E., 21
Brogan, P., 95, 124
Brown, D., 143
Bruner, J., 6
Brunner, D., 166
Brutt-Griffler, J., 162
Butt, R., 8
Byrd, B., 91

Byrd, S. M., 91

C

Campbell, G., 127, 146
Carger, C., 21
Carlson, D., 5
Casey, K., 7, 8
Castaneda, J., 91
Cervantes, R. C., 84
Cha, D., 54
Cha, S., xiii, 20, 54
Chailand, G., 124
Chan, S., 54
Cheung, S., 54
Chomsky, N., 62, 63
Clandinin, D., 6
Clark, R., 124, 155
Clausen, J., 6
Cochran-Smith, M., 4
Cockburn, A., 124
Cockburn, P., 124
Cohen, L., 146
Cole, A., 8
Connelly, F., 6
Conquergood, D., 54
Cooper, R., 35
Cortes, M. G., 26
Covello, L., 13, 169
Crapanzano, V., 6
Cremin, L., 6
Cummins, J., 14

Subject Index